Real Life Recruitment Solutions

Editor:
Mark Crail

Print on Demand Edition

Published by
Tottel Publishing Ltd
Maxwelton House
41-43 Boltro Road
Haywards Heath
West Sussex
RH16 1BJ

ISBN 13: 978-1-84592-694-6
ISBN 10: 1-84592-694-3
© Eclipse Group 2002
Formerly published by LexisNexis Butterworths

This edition reprinted by Tottel Publishing Ltd 2007

All rights reserved. No part of this publication may be reproduced in any material form (including photocopying or storing it in any medium by electronic means and whether or not transiently or incidentally to some other use of this publication) without the written permission of the copyright owner except in accordance with the provisions of the Copyright, Designs and Patents Act 1988 or under the terms of a licence issued by the Copyright Licensing Agency Ltd., 90 Tottenham Court Road, London, England W1T 4LP. Applications for the copyright owner's written permission to reproduce any part of this publication should be addressed to the publisher.

Warning: The doing of unauthorised act in relation to a copyright work may result in both a civil claim for damages and criminal prosecution.

Crown copyright material is reproduced with the permission of the Controller of HMSO and the Queen's Printer for Scotland. Parliamentary copyright material is reproduced with the permission of the Controller of Her Majesty's Stationery Office on behalf of Parliament. Any European material in this work which has been reproduced from EUR-lex, the official European Communities legislation website, is European Communities copyright.

British Library Cataloguing-in-Publication Data.
A catalogue record for this book is available from the British Library.

Production and typesetting by Brett Gamston
Printed and bound in Great Britain by
Marston Book Services, Abingdon, Oxfordshire

Contents

	Page
Introduction	1
1. Advertising for staff	3
The case for recruitment advertising	3
The case against recruitment advertising	3
Who advertises in the press?	3
Does it work?	4
Making it work for you	4
Where is the evidence?	7
Using agencies	8
Checklist	9
Case study	10
2. Online recruiting	13
The case for online recruitment	13
The case against online recruitment	13
Does the internet still matter?	13
Who uses the internet and why?	14
Lessons from the FTSE-100	15
Employing graduates	15
Help for recruiters	16
3. Employer Direct and the jobcentre network	17
The case for Employer Direct	17
The case against Employer Direct	17
Modernising jobcentres	17
Services for employers	18
The future	19
4. Employment agencies	21
The case for employment agencies	21
The case against employment agencies	21
How agencies can help	22

	Problems with agencies	22
	The changing legal picture	23
	Choosing an agency	24
	What jobs can agencies help fill?	24
	Recruiting agency temps	25
	Where problems arise	26
	A note on the law	26
	Checklist	27
5.	**Search consultants**	**29**
	The case for search consultants	29
	The case against search consultants	29
	Getting the best out of search consultants	30
	How much should you pay?	31
	Case studies	31
6.	**Employee referral payments**	**35**
	The case for bounty payments	35
	The case against bounty payments	35
	How to make a bounty scheme work	36
	How much should you pay?	37
	Case study	38
7.	**Effective application forms**	**39**
	The case for application forms	39
	The case against application forms	39
	Application forms versus CVs	39
	Making the most of application forms	40
	A note about the law	42
	Case study	44
8.	**Effective interviews**	**45**
	The case for interviews	45
	The case against interviews	45
	Choosing the right kind of interview	45
	Running successful interviews	47
	Effective interview skills	51
	Checklists	52
9.	**Telephone interviewing**	**57**
	The case for telephone interviews	57
	The case against telephone interviews	57

	Why employers use this approach	57
	How telephone interviews help	58
	Problems you may encounter	59
	Where is the evidence?	59
	Case Studies	61
10.	**Online selection**	**65**
	The case for online selection	65
	The case against online selection	65
	Early lessons from the pioneers	65
	Security and risk management	66
	Rethinking the application	67
	Points to remember	67
	Case studies	67
11.	**Psychometric testing**	**73**
	The case for psychometric testing	73
	The case against psychometric testing	73
	Who uses psychometric tests?	73
	What are employers doing?	74
	Online testing	75
	The future	76
	A note on the law	77
12.	**Assessment centres**	**81**
	The case for assessment centres	81
	The case against assessment centres	81
	What is an assessment centre	81
	Making the most of assessment centres	82
	Checklist	84
	Case studies	85
13.	**Employer references**	**93**
	The case for references	93
	The case against references	93
	How common are checks on references?	93
	Getting the most out of references	94
	Beyond the reference	96
	Do references make a difference?	97
	A note on the law	97
	Checklist	100
	Case studies	101

14. Case study – Tesco Pharmacy — 107
- Links with universities — 107
- Myths about high street pharmacy — 108
- How the company responded — 109
- Winning job advertisements — 109
- Targeting the right audience — 110
- Employer reputation — 110
- Regional recruitment — 111
- Exploring new avenues — 111
- Feedback and review — 112

15. Case study – B&Q — 113
- The challenge — 113
- The strategy — 114
- Succession and career planning — 115
- People are the tools of the trade — 115
- The future — 117

16. Case study – Virginmoney.com — 119
- The importance of brand — 119
- Using a recruitment agency — 120
- Selecting for a culture — 120
- Recommend a friend — 121
- Defining the culture — 121
- New starters — 122
- Retaining staff — 122
- Success is measurable — 123

Introduction

No other employment challenge ranks as high as that of recruiting and keeping the right people. Year after year, research by IRS finds these twin issues outstrip the problems presented by the ever-changing legal and regulatory requirements on employers, administrative red tape, or even the annual pay round.

And despite the economic downturn since the turn of the millennium, and the rising number of redundancies, particularly in the manufacturing industry, there is little indication that it will become significantly easier in the foreseeable future to find and recruit good employees. Indeed, with unemployment at its lowest level for a generation and skill shortages endemic in some sectors, the challenge may even become that bit harder.

This book aims to help employers to maximise their ability to recruit by passing on practical information drawn from our own studies of what the best employers actually do. Some of our findings are presented here as straightforward statistics – we think it can be important to know whether your own practices put you in the majority or in a small minority. Others are contained in case studies based on named employers – among them well known names such as the computer manufacturer Hewlett-Packard, coffee shop chain Pret A Manger and high street bank Abbey National. There are public sector organisations here too, such as Lewisham Council, Royal Surrey County Hospital NHS Trust and the National Portrait Gallery. Each of these case studies illustrates one facet of the recruitment process and provides a useful reality check on an area of employment where theory abounds.

The book itself is divided into 16 chapters. Each of the first 13 chapters looks at a different aspect of recruitment, from advertising to interviewing and psychometric testing. Each chapter has easy-to-follow summaries of the strengths and weaknesses of the subject under examination and advice on how to make the most of the opportunities on offer. Where appropriate, there are checklists to help you ensure you miss nothing.

Our final three chapters provide more detailed case studies setting out how three companies with strong corporate brands are dealing with different recruitment challenges.

Much of the research on which this book is based was originally published in *IRS Employment Review* and its sister title, *Employee Development Bulletin*, But we have also gone further to examine evidence collected by other reputable organisations and tell you what it means. This research is fully referenced and sourced should you wish to find out more.

Introduction

In summary, our aim is to deliver precisely what we say on the front cover: real life recruitment solutions.

Mark Crail
Editor

Chapter 1
Advertising for staff

Employers invest well over £1 billion a year in advertising for staff. As with all investments, care, knowledge and expertise, plus some luck, are required if the investment is to pay good dividends. But recruitment advertising tends to fall unhappily into the category of techniques that suffer from over-familiarity. Apart from the annual mutual back-slapping of award ceremonies, there has been little investigation of what works and why.

This chapter explains how employers use recruitment advertising and whether it is effective. It looks in some detail about how employers can design their recruitment advertising campaign to best effect, using evidence obtained by IRS and through academic studies. And it concludes with guidance on the use of recruitment advertising agencies, including a case study of brewer Greene King's use of an agency in employer branding.

THE CASE FOR RECRUITMENT ADVERTISING

- It is a quick and easy way to reach potential employees.

- It can be targeted on the right audience at the right time.

- It is proven to work.

THE CASE AGAINST RECRUITMENT ADVERTISING

- Your advert may be competing against hundreds of similar postings.

- You may not want to reveal details – such as salary – that help to attract candidates.

- It may not be appropriate for very senior or specialist posts where the requirements mean there will be only a handful of suitable candidates.

WHO ADVERTISES IN THE PRESS?

According to the Chartered Institute of Personnel and Development[1], 86.6% of employers turn to the local press, 80.2% to a specialist publication and 71.5% to a national newspaper when they have a managerial, professional or skilled-manual vacancy to fill. By comparison, 66% of employers use employment agencies.

DOES IT WORK?

The British are inveterate newspaper readers so it is no surprise that print media – national newspapers, local press, trade magazines, specialist journals and the like – are heavily used to publicise job opportunities. But many employers are reluctant to put all their eggs in one basket, and often explore other ways of finding good-quality staff alongside their advertising? So, is the huge use of the press merely a recruiter's habit?

One study based on interviews with 1,188 employers found that press advertisements represented the largest single source of successful applicants – that is, those who were actually hired from among all those who came forward – generating a quarter of successful applicants. And employers of all sizes shared much the same experience of the effectiveness of press advertising.

MAKING IT WORK FOR YOU

Where should you advertise?

A recruitment advertisement is no more than an invitation to apply for a vacancy. Choosing the right medium is a question of balancing cost and audience. At the risk of over-simplification, the choice is usually made in this way:

- For vacancies that are sufficiently highly paid to justify the expense of moving house, choose from among the national broadsheets. This source provides access to a level of the labour market that cuts across geographical boundaries. Each paper tends to specialise in certain types of vacancy, and may vary its focus from day to day – so that the Monday edition might be devoted to public sector appointments while the Tuesday edition concentrates on vacancies for academic and related staff. Though advertising in the national press is expensive, the alternatives (headhunters or specialist agencies) are more expensive still.

- For occupations whose incumbents identify themselves as having a common set of interests, or who constitute a profession in their own right, there is often a suitable specialist, trade or professional title (for example, for nurses, architects or engineers). Specialist publications are often national in their coverage but charge less than broadsheet newspapers.

- For relatively low-paid vacancies, or for those with insufficient specialisation to have their own trade journal, local newspapers are usually most suitable. Big cities and some more rural counties have daily morning or evening newspapers, but in many other areas the principal local newspapers will be weekly.

Personal knowledge may be all that is required to identify the publications most relevant to a particular vacancy. Alternatively, or additionally, those working in the same part of the organisation as the post being filled will usually have a shrewd idea of the best sources of job advertisements. Newspapers and magazines displayed in libraries, the media directories they may have in their reference collections, and searching the internet can be additional sources of inspiration when selecting appropriate media.

One of the key sources for those involved in several recruitment exercises each year is the media directory BRAD[2]. It has more than 13,000 entries, some of which are updated in each monthly issue.

What should the advert say?

The ideal job advertisement will grab the attention of a casual reader who may not even be actively looking for a new post, but generate a few good-quality applicants, minimising the time and cost involved in recruitment. Unfortunately, there is no one accepted best way of baiting the hook.

One school of thought argues that informative adverts with prominent job titles and some good background information on the vacancy and its requirements will succeed in attracting attention. Others believe that striking or unusual advertisements work best – perhaps utilising colour and an eye-catching statement or graphic to make it stand out.

There are some points, though, from research into the elements of job ads that contribute to successful recruiting. One study[3] analysed more than 9,000 recruitment advertisements published in a single month. It found that: "Employers who 'invested' more money in the advertisement by specifying a greater number of skills tend to receive more applications for the job, and are more likely to have obtained all the skills, qualifications and experience that they require."

According to Wickland Westcott[4], a selection, assessment and development consultancy: "Research shows that potential candidates are drawn first to the job title, then to the salary indicator and, finally, to the location. If these three criteria broadly meet their expectations, then the rest of the copy will be scanned to see what scope the job offers. At this point, any entry requirements are probably noted and a mental tally done of matching experience."

The Executive Search and Selection division of the PricewaterhouseCoopers consultancy asked almost 1,400 senior managers and directors what they considered to be the vital elements in recruitment advertisements that might attract them to apply[5].

They confirmed Wickland Westcott's assertion that the job title is the most important factor for jobseekers at this senior level, closely followed by salary. "These factors are much more important than the size and position of the advertisement, or whether the ad is in colour or includes pictures or graphics," the survey's report says.

Should you mention salary?

Recommendations based on best-practice research usually suggest including details about salary and benefits in recruitment advertisements. It is evident, though, that many employers disagree, as their advertisements omit such details.

In such cases, however, "attractive salary" is in danger of being understood to mean: "As it's so low, it's attractive to us".

While few jobseekers begin their job search because they want higher pay - most are prompted by dissatisfaction with the way they are managed or denied development - few will be attracted to a new position if the salary is lower than their present one. Denying potential applicants this key piece of information is likely to handicap recruiters by discouraging some potentially suitable people from applying.

However, recruiters seldom enjoy complete autonomy. Many organisations, particularly those with performance-related pay, keep salary levels confidential within the organisation and are, therefore, unlikely to allow disclosure outside it. A compromise of quoting a salary range may be possible, though.

Alternatively, the absence of a salary tag may be no more than a reflection that a recruiter has accurately targeted the market for a vacancy.

Keeping candidates informed

As well as contact details, potential applicants need to know how the employer intends to handle their application. Some employers use telephone-screening interviews as an initial step, some expect candidates to compose a letter of application, some will accept standard CVs, while others rely on application forms. The dividing lines between these different approaches are not always clear to applicants and should be spelled out.

The practice of giving a contact telephone number in job advertisements has increased in recent years. Making a phone call to obtain an application form or background information is fast, convenient and an opportunity to make some informal contact. Provided that the experience gives a friendly and efficient impression, this can help in the process of developing the "psychological contract" with the new employee.

For more senior jobs, particularly, the contact details may include an offer to telephone someone who can discuss the job with applicants – often the line manager, and sometimes the incumbent if they are still in post.

The inclusion of a website address adds a further and potentially much larger dimension to a recruitment advertisement. Corporate websites invariably contain information that could help a potential applicant, giving background details and information on corporate values.

WHERE IS THE EVIDENCE?

Karel De Witte's research[6] into the factors involved in effective recruitment advertising is frequently cited as an important source of information on the positioning, design and content of such adverts. The research was carried out some time ago (in the 1980s) and in another country (Belgium), so its findings are probably of most use today in highlighting the issues that recruiters should address for themselves.

By interviewing 400 potential job applicants De Witte's found out what elements of a recruitment advertisement jobseekers attached most importance to. Ranked from most to least important these turned out to be:

- the job's functional requirements;

- job title and location;

- the name of the organisation;

- whether the postholder would be required to live near the workplace;

- the pay and benefits package;

- characteristics of the organisation;

- information about the selection process;

- size of organisation; and

- whether psychometric testing was to be used in selection.

The way jobseekers scanned newspaper jobs pages was also investigated, by observing their eye movements. The job title was very important. It "seems to be the element to decide on to move to the next advertisement, and not the organisation."

Another project analysed 800 recruitment advertisements in a national newspaper for their position on the page, style, content and layout. After each advertisement had appeared, the employer was asked how many useful responses it had generated.

This project found that:

- it is not true that the position of an advertisement on a particular page or the place within a page is very important; but

- the size of the advertisement "has a significant influence on the number of responses";

- the amount of information about pay and benefits has a significant influence on the number of responses (more information, more responses);

- the use of colour will produce more responses, if most other advertisements are in black and white; and

- information about the employer and the job's requirements proves useful in self-selection, encouraging applicants who are more suited to the vacancy and discouraging others.

Based on the results of these and other projects, De Witte found that:

- potential applicants scan pages of job advertisements, and find it easiest to identify a particular advert when it is "well-structured" and has some ready means of being recognised; then

- they focus on the name of the organisation and the job title to make a decision about whether to stop their scanning and read a particular advertisement; and

- at this point, readers expect extensive information about the functional requirements, and seek information about the organisation.

- if the information matches what they want, they will read on.

USING AGENCIES

Why use an agency?

Producing a cost-effective advertisement is no easy matter, so it is not surprising that many employers turn to agencies for advice. When IRS surveyed 102 employers in 2002, we found that four out of five used an agency to help fill at least some vacancies[7].

The fortunes of recruitment advertising agencies are particularly sensitive to the ebb and flow of the economy, so a downturn often leads to restructuring in the industry. However, the main industry body, the Institute for Practitioners in Advertising, divides its members into two categories:

- **full-service agencies** dealing with everything from employer branding to campaign planning and advert placement; and

- **media specialists** principally advising on the choice of media and placing the advertisement.

What do other employers do?

The IRS study found that employers principally want their agency to handle the technical side of recruitment advertising – identifying suitable media and placing the advertisement, with few expecting it to handle initial responses.

The agency services most commonly used by employers are:

- identifying suitable publications/media   88%
- advising on graphics/presentation   75%
- negotiating media discounts   75%
- advising on text of advertisements   54%
- writing text of advertisements   44%
- handling initial responses   12%

CHECKLIST

Choosing and using an agency

If you decide to choose an agency, you will need to plan ahead to get the most out of the arrangement. Employers taking part in the IRS study mentioned above give this advice:

- Determine which services are required, and set them out in detail in the tender document or background papers.

- Decide whether the contract will cover all vacancies or just some, and what criteria you will use to identify eligible vacancies.

- Select factors that will determine your choice of agency, and their relative performance – some of this information will be useful to agencies bidding for the contract as it clarifies your expectations.

- Agree on the relationship you want with the agency – will it emphasise compliance and control, or long-term partnership?

- Provide full information and briefings about your organisation's culture, business activities and types of vacancies – up-to-date job descriptions and person specifications are important.

- Brief the agency on the minimum selection criteria the employer will use.

- Establish in advance how the agency's performance is to be assessed, and communicate this to the agency – formal performance monitoring may require benchmarking data against which the agency can be compared.

CASE STUDY

Greene King opts for employer branding

Brewer and public house owner Greene King awarded its brewing, brands and wholesaling account to recruitment advertising agency aia. The work involves the development of an employer brand, a house style and a standard advertising manual, alongside more traditional services such as copywriting and the placement of advertisements in appropriate media.

Green King awarded the account to aia after a three-way fight. As the brewery's human resource manager, Louise Sinclair, explains, it chose the agency because its "approach was straightforward and innovative and we have no doubt that it will be a successful working relationship. We chose aia because we could relate to them as a company and they were very much values led."

Val Moore, aia's joint managing director, says the agency's role will also be "to set standards and create an easily identifiable look and feel that will attract dynamic fresh thinkers to complement its existing team of loyal, dedicated staff". The agency offers clients a range of related services, from graduate recruitment brochures and mainstream recruitment advertising to employee communications and response management.

CHECKLIST

Potential pitfalls

Watch out for these possible problem areas with your agency:

- **Customer focus:** an agency may give insufficient attention to the job by failing to ensure continuity of staff handling the account, not giving time and attention to understand your requirements or by being unreceptive to feedback.

- **Timeliness:** there may be delays in responding, a failure to produce copy on time or missed publication deadlines.

- **Quality of copy:** dangers include factual errors, typographical mistakes, a poor reflection of the vacancy's requirements or poor layout and design.

- **Costs:** advertisements may be larger and more costly than agreed, discounts may not have been negotiated or passed on.

- **Creativity versus practicality:** beware of a failure to get the balance right – being too creative at the expense of practicality, or, conversely, lacking ideas and flair.

- **Media knowledge:** has the agency selected the most suitable media, particularly for specialist or hard-to-fill vacancies?

- **Commitment:** has the agency's commitment waned since the contract was awarded?

- **Administration:** inaccurate or tardy administration – in particular, failing to provide accurate invoices – is a danger sign.

Sources

1. "Recruitment survey report", Chartered Institute of Personnel and Development, May 2001.

2. www.brad.co.uk.

3. "Central London jobs and skills: a biannual review", Focus Central London Training and Enterprise Council, 2000.

4. Wickland Westcott Bulletin, Autumn 1998.

5. Top jobs recruitment advertising survey, PricewaterhouseCoopers, 1999.

6. "Recruiting and advertising", Karel De Witte, chapter 2.4 in "Assessment and selection in organizations", edited by Peter Herriot, John Wiley, 1989.

7. "Putting on a brave face" published in two parts in *IRS Employment Review* 738, October 2001, and 739, November 2001; and "Make-up artists", *IRS Employment Review* 745, February 2002.

Chapter 2
Online recruiting

The internet has transformed the way many people look for a new job. Easy access means that students searching for their first job can find out quickly and easily about potential employers, while the ubiquitous office PC allows many people in work to browse job sites even when they are not actively looking to move on – vastly increasing the potential audience for those looking to fill vacancies.

This chapter looks at lasting legacy of the dotcom revolution and its dotbomb aftermath for recruiters, examining recent trends in employers' use of online recruitment and investigating the ways in which large companies use their corporate websites to attract new talent through their doors.

THE CASE FOR ONLINE RECRUITMENT

- It is cheap – both in absolute cost terms and per job filled.

- The administrative burden of recruiting online has been over-emphasised.

- It is increasingly expected, particularly by graduates looking for their first job.

THE CASE AGAINST ONLINE RECRUITMENT

- There is little evidence that it produces more or better candidates.

- Not every potentially successful recruit will have internet access.

- Employers may not have the infrastructure to cope.

DOES THE INTERNET STILL MATTER?

After the early goldrush years when it appeared to many that the internet offered not simply another medium of communication but the basis of a whole new economy, the proliferation of job websites attempting either to accumulate as many vacancies as possible or to specialise in particular industries and sectoral niches has now come to an end and the number of sites has reduced.

There have, however, been a number of success stories – often involving sites linked to companies already operating in the recruitment field, such as the Guardian Media

Group's *Workthing* website, and TMP Worldwide recruitment agency's Monsterboard. And the face of graduate recruitment may have changed irreversibly thanks to the high level of IT literacy and ready access to the internet in higher education. According to research carried out by IRS[1], three out of four FTSE-100 companies use the internet in one way or another in their recruitment process, and many other large employers have followed suit. Among big employers, online recruitment is now the norm not the exception.

Some smaller sites with a tighter focus on particular industries and professions also appear to be doing well – though such is the fragile state of what was once the "new economy" that even now it is difficult to predict their long-term future. However, with the number of people using the internet to look for jobs increasing by 50% during 2001, and with nine out of 10 personnel and HR practitioners expecting to increase their online recruitment during 2002[2], it would be a brave decision to opt out of the e-revolution.

WHO USES THE INTERNET AND WHY?

Three out of five larger employers have some experience of using the internet to recruit staff, and although manufacturers are less likely to have done so than those in either the public or private sector services, research by IRS has established that most medium and large-sized organisations are fairly familiar with web-based recruitment to some extent[3].

A separate study by IRS found that three out of four FTSE-100 companies used their own corporate websites to recruit new staff, with others turning to job boards, handing over the responsibility for online recruitment to external suppliers.

However, now that greater experience is available, there are signs that the claimed benefits of online recruitment are coming under greater scrutiny. For example, while the internet is commonly accepted as being a relatively blunt instrument – leading to more unsuitable job applications being received – many recruiters also believe it is no better than traditional methods in increasing the overall number of applicants.

On the plus side, the technical challenges of administering electronic forms of recruitment do not seem to represent a widespread problem. Most believe the administrative burden is no greater or worse than that posed by paper-based routines. And the internet really comes into its own on issues of cost.

Most employers also report that it less expensive than traditional approaches – both when measured as an absolute cost, and when calculated on the basis of the number of successful appointments made.

Among large employers surveyed by IRS who had no plans to use their websites, the following reasons were given:

- online recruitment will be of no use to the organisation;

- the investment required to make effective use of the internet would be too heavy for the organisation to justify or bear; and

- the organisation does not have an appropriate infrastructure in place to support an online recruitment function within the personnel department.

LESSONS FROM THE FTSE-100

While most smaller employers will want to use job boards to reach potential candidates, very large and very well known companies can make use of their own websites, secure in the knowledge that people know of their existence and will actively seek out opportunities to work for them.

Any attempt to follow this route, however, will be effective only if jobseekers can find the recruitment site or section of the corporate website and use it without too many problems. And while most FTSE-100 companies investigated by IRS clearly linked from their home page to a page listed as "job opportunities", "careers" or "recruitment", some included it within sections "about us" or in "company profile" pages. While this may seem logical to the organisations when developing their websites, it may not appear so to jobseekers who have less interest in the history or structure of the company.

All the websites had some information about the company's culture or working environment. This is important as it gives applicants an opportunity to find out more about the organisation and begin to self select. The Royal Bank of Scotland, for example, includes the following statement: "If you are seeking to work in a 'traditional' banking environment, then may we suggest that your next click takes you out of this site. But if you want to know more about working for an organisation that has broken the mould, then click on the lefthand-side navigation."

EMPLOYING GRADUATES

Graduate recruitment has moved further online than most. Every website from the FTSE-100 companies that we looked at had particular mention of graduate recruitment or a specific section for them. Two organisations had separate websites for the recruitment of graduates.

One benefit of this special attention is the ability to direct graduates straight to this section, which can be custom built to appeal to them. The style and language used can be different and less sober than that used in main corporate sites, where investors and prospective investors will expect to see business-focused, results-driven information.

The use of case studies is also prevalent. Organisations have put together case details of previous graduates and how they have succeeded in the company. All of which is useful information to new graduates researching their career alternatives on leaving university or college.

Organisations that recruit graduates regularly are aware that this group make a high level of applications when they have left university and are looking for work. The internet is, therefore, an effective way for organisations to carry out some initial pre-screening.

One in 10 of the FTSE-100 organisations that are using their corporate websites in recruitment are using pre-screening in the graduate section to ensure that all application forms they receive are relevant, and that graduates are serious about applying. It also ensures that only eligible applicants begin the process. Anglo American, GKN, ICI, Abbey National, PowerGen, Marks & Spencer and BT Group use this facility. Generally, the screening process asks graduates about the quality of degree they expect to receive; eligibility to work in the UK and number of UCAS points. There is more about the use of the internet in selection in Chapter 10.

HELP FOR RECRUITERS

Many organisations are emerging to help support recruiters who are using the internet.

- The **Association of Online Recruiters** is part of the Recruitment and Employment Confederation. It can be found at www.aolr.org.uk. Organisations that join the association must abide by its code of practice.

- The **Association for Internet Recruiting** is American based and can be found at www.recruitersnetwork.com.

Sources

1. "Internet recruiting the FTSE-100 way", *IRS Employment Review* 746, February 2002.

2. People Management online, Research Centre, 23 October 2001, www.peoplemanagement.co.uk/archiveitem.asp?id=1408.

3. "Employers pessimistic about an end to their resourcing problems", *IRS Employment Review* 751, May 2002.

Chapter 3
Employer Direct and the jobcentre network

The Employment Service and its jobcentre network is not always the first port of call for employers wishing to advertise vacancies. But the government aims to tackle this problem through a wide-ranging reorganisation, including a new initiative, Employer Direct. This sets out to provide "a highly professional vacancy-taking service" as part of a comprehensive recruitment facility. Importantly, the Employer Direct service, aimed at employers looking for employees, is now run separately from the service available to jobseekers.

This chapter looks at the new service being offered to employers and sets out some of the government's future modernisation plans.

THE CASE FOR EMPLOYER DIRECT

- It is free.

- Multi-million pound government investment has created a fast and flexible service.

- A single contact point for employers and the separation of services for employers from those for jobseekers makes the service more responsive.

THE CASE AGAINST EMPLOYER DIRECT

- The Employment Service has little history of success in dealing with senior vacancies, and as yet still only has plans to develop such a service.

- The centralisation of services for employers may mean that those dealing with vacancies have little or no knowledge of local labour market conditions.

MODERNISING JOBCENTRES

The past two years have seen a far-reaching modernisation programme within the Employment Service, made possible by a huge investment in new technology. Online recruitment and call centre systems have been introduced to streamline the services available for both employers and jobseekers.

As part of its approach to moving people from welfare to work, the government is introducing a "demand-led service" for employers using jobcentres, helping them to "find the right people to fill their jobs, quickly and successfully".

Available in 50 "pathfinder" offices since October 2001, the new service aims to respond strategically to the labour requirements of employers in different sectors and areas of the country. A partnership approach to working with employers has been adopted, with local account managers providing a tailored service to meet individual organisations' needs. The intention is to provide a more professional recruitment service, based on improved communications and "the full range of channels offered by modern technology".

In 2001, the jobcentre network was responsible for placing 1.3 million people in work. Jobcentre Plus will not only advertise vacancies nationwide and on the internet, but also distribute application forms, screen suitable candidates and help with interviews, all free of charge. Vacant posts can also be advertised abroad by passing details to other public employment services in the EU.

SERVICES FOR EMPLOYERS

Employer Direct is the new, centralised service for employers provided by Jobcentre Plus. Before the creation of the new agency, around 700 of the 1,000 jobcentres throughout the country were responsible for dealing with local employer vacancies. Now, a call to the single, low-cost, national telephone number (0845 601 2001) or a fax (020 8285 8007) or email (employerservices@ jobcentreplus.gov.uk) enables employers to notify their vacancies, and kickstarts the recruitment advertising process.

Within minutes of the employer contacting Employer Direct, the vacancy is entered into an internet Job Bank so that details of the vacancy are instantly accessible across the country via the government's two employment websites and from new "jobpoints". These are "easy-to-use, touch-screen kiosks", where jobseekers can obtain information about vacancies. More than 9,000 jobpoints have replaced the old job vacancy boards in jobcentres. As a person looking for work can call up job details for any part of the UK, this new facility means that potentially an employer is casting a much wider recruitment net.

The Department for Work and Pensions, which is responsible for Jobcentre Plus, believes that providing a single contact point for employers to place their vacancies will produce a more responsive and faster service, vital to meeting employers' recruitment needs today.

The infrastructure to support Employer Direct involved establishing a network of 11 regional customer service centres. The call centres are staffed predominantly by employees who have trained with the Employment Service. Between March and December 2001, the new centres fielded around 875,000 enquiries on the national telephone helpline.

As well as recording vacancy details, staff monitor subsequent recruitment activity. A named call centre contact makes a follow-up call to an employer two weeks after a vacant post has been notified to check progress on recruitment. If the employer is not satisfied with the level of interest shown in the post, the call centre employee will contact the employer's local jobcentre for help in filling the vacancy.

Step by step

Employer Direct is open for longer than standard office hours (8am to 8pm, Monday to Friday and 10am to 4pm on Saturday) and, if notifying their vacancies by fax or by email, employers can make use of the service around the clock. When an employer telephones the national number, an adviser records the job details using a computer-assisted scripted process. The basic information requested includes job title, place of work, duties to be performed, experience/qualifications required, personal qualities needed, preferred method of application and contact details.

THE FUTURE

Executive and professional posts

The modernisation programme for the Employment Service includes ES Plus Online, "an extra service for employers with executive and professional vacancies". Jobcentres have traditionally found it difficult to convince employers that they can handle this higher level of job vacancy effectively. The pilot scheme covering the South West will aim to put employers in touch with unemployed executives and professionals who want to get back into work. A small team of people will screen candidates for suitability and "only pass on the best", at no direct cost to the employer.

The government has invested millions of pounds in transforming the jobcentre network and the services it provides for employers. Whether or not the new services will match those offered by the commercial recruitment sector remains to be seen, but, as they are available free of charge, employers have little to lose by finding out.

Internet job banking

Jobcentre Plus's central database holds details of around 300,000 vacancies at any one time. These vacancies can now be accessed "24 hours a day, seven days a week" via the agency's two websites by jobseekers and employers alike. The agency plans to provide an internet route for employers to manage their own vacancies online in the near future, and has already piloted such a scheme. If implemented, this will be a significant development for employers. As well as the instant and highly accessible nature of the service, it will enable employers to take control of the recruitment process. Not only will an employer be able to notify new vacancies online, it will have the facility to input any changes to existing ones.

Anyone actively looking for work who has access to a computer can search online for suitable vacancies, although, at the moment, applications must still be made through a jobcentre. This may change soon, though. It is also planned that employers will be able to search for candidates' CVs online. Jobseekers will be able to input details of their career history, skills and the type of work they are looking for into a CV Bank. Employers can then conduct their own search for suitable job candidates. Other plans include the intention to alert jobseekers by email to specific vacancies if it is felt that they have the suitable skills and experience for the job. This means that jobcentres will actively promote employers' vacancies, but in a targeted fashion.

Chapter 4
Employment agencies

The UK is unusual in having a large and influential job-placement service under private ownership. In some European countries, private agencies were banned for many years and often continue to be strictly controlled. Here, while the state-owned network of jobcentres is often seen as competing effectively at the lower end of the labour market, commercial agencies have established a very strong position for other types of worker. The Department of Trade and Industry estimates that employers pay some £18 billion a year to agencies[1], and as well as supplying recruits, commercial agencies are often the first port of call for employers wishing to make use of temporary workers of all types.

In this chapter we look how the advantages and disadvantages of using employment agencies, set out the results of IRS research into how employers choose and use agencies, and touch on ways in which changes in the law will affect employers' use of agencies. There is also a detailed checklist of points to watch when choosing and using an employment agency.

THE CASE FOR EMPLOYMENT AGENCIES

- They have access to a pool of jobseekers that they can draw upon as soon as an employer contacts them.
- They can help meet temporary needs in a cost-efficient way that avoids many legal complications.
- They offer a way of trying out temporary staff who may later become permanent employees.

THE CASE AGAINST EMPLOYMENT AGENCIES

- Some employers have encountered problems with over-charging and inflated costs.
- Many agencies lack the specific industry knowledge needed to meet employers' needs.
- Ensuring that an agency gets the balance right between suitably qualified and sufficient numbers of candidates can be a struggle.

HOW AGENCIES CAN HELP

For employers, the appeal of agencies' temping services lies in their potential to provide stop-gap staff at short notice. They provide cover for absences, offer skills where only a temporary need exists or where vacancies are unfilled because of recruitment problems, and avoid the legal complications of direct recruitment by the employer. Such staff are either employees of the agency or are self-employed.

Permanent recruitment through agencies offers several advantages, depending on the vacancy. In some occupations, agencies are jobseekers' preferred route into new permanent jobs, and thus employers gain best access to these segments of the labour market through the use of an agency. In other cases, agencies act as a backstop where vacancies prove difficult to fill through employers' own efforts. The agency might have job seekers on its books, or uncover other potential candidates through advertising or the use of online recruitment.

More generally, agencies can help employers improve their recruitment by shortening the lead times involved. Where they can supply potential recruits from their books, employers may be able to avoid time-consuming and costly recruitment advertising to provide a field of candidates.

PROBLEMS WITH AGENCIES
Too much choice

Employers face a bewildering choice of agencies. Back in the mid-1990s there were some 11,950 agency offices in the UK, and there has been sustained growth since then. The sheer number of agencies makes the selection of a supplier a difficult, time-consuming matter. Nor is the agency industry well organised at present, so employers cannot draw up a shortlist of potential suppliers by contacting a single representative body. Even the best known, the Recruitment and Employment Confederation, is estimated by the government to cover no more than 50% of all agencies.

Nor do most agencies specialise in supplying temporary workers or helping to recruit permanent employees – even though many focus on a particular locality, industry, occupation, or a combination of these.

High costs and complex charges

Agencies' charges tend to involve complex cost structures. Even the seemingly straightforward process of supplying temporary workers can involve various permutations of charges and penalty clauses. The hourly/daily/weekly rate, for example, may be based on the typical short-term demands of employers, but, where a longer-term need is identified, it may be possible to negotiate a reduction in charges. Generally, though, as recruitment expert Stephen Taylor points out: "Hourly rates for agency workers are invariably double those paid to regular employees."[2]

Interim management commands particularly high rates. This is a specialised form of temporary work involving executives who provide managerial expertise to companies.

Frequently, an agency's contract for the supply of temporary workers will also impose a charge should the employer then recruit the person as a permanent member of staff. Research for the government found that four out of five agencies imposed such a charge, and shows that those which do so generally adopt one of two approaches:

- straight commission based on salary (used by 58% of agencies and averaging 15% of pay); or
- combination of commission and flat fee (used by the remaining 42% of agencies).

The arrangements for charges in respect of agencies' role in permanent recruitment are even more variable and complex than is the case in their provision of temps. Depending on the level/status of the vacancy, and the type of service required, an agency may charge a straight commission, based on a proportion of the job's annual salary, an overall fee (perhaps paid in stages), or some other arrangement. Typically, an agency might charge 10%–13% of the annual salary of the post being filled – though this would include an initial visit to the employer, handling responses to a recruitment advertisement or recruitment website, initial telephone interviews and drawing up a shortlist.

THE CHANGING LEGAL PICTURE

Two legal developments, unprecedented in their potential impact on the use of agencies, are about to shake up this marketplace. First, the government has published its final proposals for changes to the legal regulation of agencies[3]. New Regulations, due to come into force in the first half of 2003, will limit agencies' ability to levy transfer fees on employers that recruit temporary workers from them, and require them to improve their selection and screening of temps and potential recruits.

Even more significantly, a forthcoming EU Directive[4] could lead to major changes in the use of temporary agency workers in three to four years' time. Under the terms of the draft Directive, agency temps would have to be given pay, holidays, hours of work and other conditions equal to those of permanent members of staff doing similar work in the same organisation. It is also possible that, instead of controlling transfer fees (also known as "temp-to-perm fees") as the domestic legislation will do, the Directive may completely ban them.

The result of the Directive may be higher agency fees, a reduction in employers' use of temps and a shake-out of agency businesses.

CHOOSING AN AGENCY

Employers rely on what they know when choosing an agency. Research conducted by IRS[5] found that the proven effectiveness of an agency is of paramount importance (a factor cited by 91% of the employers). And where they are not personally familiar with an agency, half of all employers will consider its reputation when deciding which firm to use.

Both of these factors assume that the agency has a track record that a potential client-employer can use as a guide to present and future standards of service. However, the high turnover of staff in many agencies, particularly during the hiring boom of recent years, means that service levels provided in the past cannot always be maintained. And the one in six agencies that are newcomers to the industry each year will not have the reputation and service record on which to base this judgment.

A third factor, in terms of the criteria used by employers to select an agency, involves employers actively matching their requirements against those that an agency can offer. Half of employers take account of an agency's specialist expertise in their own industry, in the local labour market, in the occupation(s) that the employer is interested in, or a combination of these considerations.

Cost represents a major discriminating factor, and four in 10 employers take it into consideration. Interestingly, it is of more concern to employers in their choice of a particular employment agency than it is in terms of their choice of agency to conduct their recruitment advertising.

WHAT JOBS CAN AGENCIES HELP FILL?

Employers often use agencies to supply temporary workers for certain types of job – particularly, clerical, secretarial, nursing, care and computing staff – but use agencies for different types of job when they wish to recruit permanent workers. As figure 1, below, shows, employers are more likely to use an agency to recruit managers to permanent roles than to temporary work, and turn to an agency more often for temporary rather than permanent clerical staff.

Differences exist between different types of employer, too. In particular, employers in the public sector generally follow their private sector counterparts' use of temporary workers, but change their approach in respect of filling permanent vacancies. For example, 97% of the public sector employers IRS contacted use agencies for clerical and secretarial staff to provide temporary cover, and 85% of private sector firms do so. But only 12% of the public sector fills its permanent positions for clerical and secretarial staff through agencies, against 65% of the private sector. Such differences are almost certainly due to the public sector's emphasis on public, open recruitment, usually through advertising, causing it to avoid agencies as they obtain candidates from many sources, often via self-referral.

Figure 1: Using agencies for temporary and permanent recruits

	% of employers	
Type of job	Temporary	Permanent
Managers	31	65
Professionals (lawyers, teachers, doctors)	57	66
Associate professionals (nurses, technicians, artists)	51	53
Personal services (hairdressers, care assistants)	20	6
Sales	20	27
Clerical and secretarial	89	46
Craft and skilled manufacturing	28	16
Operatives and assembly workers	34	12

RECRUITING AGENCY TEMPS

In theory, the use of temporary workers supplied by an agency provides an ideal probationary period in which to judge their performance and consider offering them a permanent position, should one arise.

However, apart from any equal opportunities considerations, two obstacles stand in the way of this approach. First, many employers need more temporary agency staff than they have permanent vacancies they need to fill. So, opportunities are often relatively uncommon. And second, agencies are concerned that employers will "cream off" their best temps, and use agencies as an unpaid recruitment service. As a result, most agencies insert clauses in their contracts with employers that impose a financial penalty known as a transfer, or temp-to-perm, fee.

Nevertheless, it seems that many employers are not deterred. Among the employers taking part in an IRS study of this area, 90% offer at least some of their permanent vacancies to temps supplied by an agency. Surprisingly, the public sector is not averse to using this route – 79% do so – despite its far lower incidence of using agencies in a direct way to help with its recruitment of permanent staff. This percentage compares with 92% of manufacturers and 97% of private sector services firms.

WHERE PROBLEMS ARISE

More than half the employers taking part in IRS research that had used agencies have encountered difficulties, although the public sector is markedly more satisfied (only 31% of users have experienced problems) than either manufacturers (62%) or, in particular, private sector services firms (74%). The reasons for these differences are unclear – possibly the public sector's emphasis on using agencies for temporary cover, rather than permanent recruits, restricts its exposure to problems.

Among the main problems encountered by employers are:

- agencies that send too many unsuitable candidates – or that adhere too tightly to the person requirements and send too few candidates or none at all;

- agencies that fail to brief jobseekers about the organisation or the job;

- agencies whose staff fail to absorb the basic information they are given about the organisation and its requirements; and

- agencies whose bills are inflated through charges not made clear in advance or through "error".

However, employers sometimes seem to expect the impossible. Where skills are in short supply, even the best agency will struggle to meet employers' demands. In fact, some employers welcomed some honesty; if an agency cannot provide an exact match, they would prefer that they were told of this and be given the chance to consider the individuals on that basis.

A NOTE ON THE LAW

Permanent recruits supplied by an agency enjoy the same legal status and protection as other employees, and actions both of employers and agencies acting as their agents are covered. The role of agencies as "gatekeepers" in the recruitment process of both temporary and permanent workers causes particular concern in terms of its significance for equal opportunities, and there have been several investigations into agencies by the relevant statutory bodies in Great Britain. The Commission for Racial Equality, for example, pays special attention to agencies in its employment Code of Practice.

Employers using temporary workers from an agency, as well as the agencies themselves, are required under existing legislation to ensure workers' health and safety and not to discriminate unfairly against them. The national minimum wage and the 1998 Working Time Regulations also apply to such workers.

Temporary workers' employment status has been unclear and, with it, the respective rights and responsibilities of employer and employee (and of self-employed persons). One of the main purposes of the Conduct of Employment Agencies and Employment Business Regulations is to clarify the legal position of the employer. The Regulations replace outdated 1976 legislation, and are expected to take effect around May 2003. Several sections will be phased in over three months after that date, including provisions relating to transfer fees.

CHECKLIST

Points to watch

Choice

- Identify the factors that will determine the choice of agency, and their relative performance. Identify where and how using an agency will offer a more cost-effective service than using internal resources.

Relationship

- Decide the desired form of relationship with the successful agency: where it will lie on a scale of shorter-term compliance and control at one end, or a longer-term partnership at the other.

- Give time and attention to establishing and maintaining good communication with the agency, including regular meetings, providing frank but constructive feedback, and openness. Productive, informed relationships are easiest to develop where one or a few agency personnel offer continuity of service to the employer.

- Provide full information and briefings about the employer's culture, business activities and types of work required of recruits and temporary workers. For permanent recruitment, provide job descriptions, person specifications and key selection criteria.

Agency performance

Watch out for:

- **Customer focus:** agencies giving insufficient attention to the customer by failing to ensure continuity of staff handling the account, and not giving time and attention to understanding the employer's requirements; being unreceptive to feedback on their performance; giving more priority to agency sales targets than meeting customer needs.

- **Candidate suitability:** sending temps or potential recruits who do not meet the specification; insufficient candidates; substituting quantity for quality in terms of potential recruits sent for interview.

- **Understanding:** failing to understand the employer's requirements; failing to impart these details and background information on the employer to jobseekers.

- **Timeliness:** delays in supplying staff; not meeting agreed deadlines; not being flexible and responsive where urgent staffing needs arise.

- **Costs:** inaccurate billing; overcharging; disputes over temp-to-perm fees.

- **Poaching:** recruiting the client employer's own staff as agency temps or on behalf of other employers.

Evaluation

- Establish in advance the ways in which the agency's performance is to be assessed, and communicate this to the agency, as this further clarifies the employer's expectations. Formal performance monitoring may require benchmarking data against which the agency can be compared.

- Decide whether or not equal opportunities monitoring is to be used, and, if it is, decide the extent to which the agency will be involved in monitoring.

Sources

1. *Recruitment agencies in the UK*, Ulrike Hotopp, Department of Trade and Industry, 2001, www.dti.gov.uk.

2. *Employee resourcing*, Stephen Taylor, Institute of Personnel and Development, 1998.

3. Revision of the Regulations covering the private recruitment industry: regulatory impact assessment, Department of Trade and Industry, 2001, www.dti.gov.uk. The Revision of Regulations for the private recruitment industry: regulatory impact assessment of July 2002 draws on the same research as used in 2001; this is also available at www.dti.gov.uk.

4. Proposal for a Directive of the European Parliament and of the Council on working conditions for temporary agency workers: regulatory impact assessment, Department of Trade and Industry, July 2002, www.dti.gov.uk.

5. "The go-betweens", *IRS Employment Review* 758, August 2002.

Chapter 5
Search consultants

Search consultants have many uses and can operate in a myriad of ways. At one end of the scale, search consultants or headhunters can delve into the marketplace and, through a series of complex and discreet negotiations, approach and secure the chief executive that an organisation has had its eye on for some time. Alternatively, they can become involved in a less complex way with the recruitment process, through screening initial applications or supplying applicants from its database of contacts.

Whatever the extent of their involvement, search consultants need to have, at least, an expert knowledge of the market that they operate in, excellent communication skills, integrity, competence, loyalty and accuracy. But they also need to have regular, two-way communication with the client employer, and therefore need good customer-care skills and considerable levels of project management expertise.

In this chapter, we look at ways of maximising the value added by search consultants to the recruitment process, focus on the experience of information communications and technology firm EDS and the local authority covering the London Borough of Lewisham, and talk to a senior manager with personal experience of being "headhunted for a project management post".

THE CASE FOR SEARCH CONSULTANTS

- They can bring wider market knowledge and a better range of contacts than are available in house.

- They can help distance your organisation from suggestions of "poaching" staff from competitors.

THE CASE AGAINST SEARCH CONSULTANTS

- The lack of competition among consultants makes it difficult to assess value for money or to find those with specific sector expertise.

- The heavy investment of time and effort getting consultants familiar with your organisation and its needs makes it difficult to switch consultancies.

GETTING THE BEST OUT OF SEARCH CONSULTANTS

Choosing your consultant

Deciding whether a search consultant should be involved in the recruitment process requires careful consideration. One mistake that can be made is assuming that any senior position, or any position with a certain salary level, should involve a search consultant.

The nature of the vacancy to be filled should also influence the decision on the search consultancy to be chosen. Some search organisations have a stronger reputation in a certain field, or have a good database of people to contact for hard-to-fill positions. For more senior positions, it may be a reputation in the industry itself that is required of the consultancy along with excellent networking skills and an ability to be discreet.

In the experience of Lewisham council's Tim Anderson: "You have to be very clear what you are getting. For example, you need to be sure you are clear on outcomes, how good their track record is, how they will work with the in-house recruitment team and know what happens if there is no appointment."

Briefing the search consultant

Any organisation making use of search consultants needs to think long and hard about the role consultants will play in the recruitment process, and about the post you are recruiting to. Giving a comprehensive brief to a search consultant can make a big difference to the overall search and can also set the tone for the exercise – defining whether the consultant needs to adopt a personal approach to fill senior roles, or to advertise for less senior positions. It will also affect the price.

The client employer must also develop a good relationship with the individual from the consultancy who will be taking forward the search. It is vital to establish effective communication between the search consultant and the organisation, and this can often be the lynchpin of recruiting an excellent candidate into the position. In order to facilitate this, there needs to be an infrastructure in place that promotes regular, two-way dialogue.

The search process will succeed only if it is closely monitored and there is regular, two-way communication. There can also be considerable coordination with other recruitment partners such as advertising agencies and testing and assessment specialists.

Other things to consider

The Association of Executive Search Consultants, a US-based organisation with branches in Europe, produces guidelines for companies selecting an executive search firm. These can be found in full on its website at www.aesc.org, but some of the key suggestions include:

- producing full written documentation before work starts – this should include a description of the post to be filled, the scope of services to be offered by the search consultant, a timetable for the process, a statement concerning fees and expenses, and a cancellation policy;
- taking up references on the work of the search firm, including speaking to previous or current clients;
- developing a clear understanding of how unusual situations are to be handled – for example, the later appointment of an unsuccessful candidate to another role within the client company; and
- ensuring you select an appropriate firm for the task, understanding what services are to be bought and ensuring the consultant has enough information to carry out the task.

HOW MUCH SHOULD YOU PAY?

The general rule with search consultants with regard to payment is a fee based on a percentage of the salary of the role being recruited. As well as this fee, administration costs are also normally levied. Some employers are unhappy with this approach, but a lack of competition in the market for recruitment consultants makes it dificult to assess value for money or to switch to an alternative firm.

David Mason at EDS says: "I'd like to see it much more related to the effort in doing the role with a reasonable level of profit. We're all in the business of making a profit, but just slapping a percentage rate – particularly at the higher end – can end up being 33% of the total remuneration package."

CASE STUDY

The candidate's perspective

Mairead de Blaca is a project manager with Ericsson, Ireland. But before taking up her present job, she worked in the United States, managing a project for the US Agency for International Development. "When I started looking for work in the US, it seemed that search consultants, headhunters and agencies were something that top-end executives used to be lured away from one highly paid job to another," she says.

By the time she left, things were very different. "Not only could you not conduct a job search without access to a personal computer and the internet, but search consultants are no longer the exception. There seemed to be a search consultant suitable for all types of potential positions; the problem was finding one that was the best fit for you."

Mairead feels that search consultants are one-dimensional in their approach to matching people to jobs. "While I have limited telecommunication and software experience, I have the competencies to manage projects concerned with such things. I have found search consultants reluctant to put my CV forward for such positions. I now work with a telecommunication company managing technical projects and software development projects.

"This isn't just a reflection on the search consultants, but also on organisations who are unwilling to look outside the established lines."

She believes on the evidence of her own experience that standards in Ireland, in her opinion, are below that of the United States. "In the US, my experience of search consultants was that they were more general and had more contact across various industries. In Ireland, many of the search consultants are not technical or have a good enough understanding of the industry or role they are recruiting for.

"Generally, I found they would latch on to buzz words within my CV and promote these. In some cases, my CV would be passed on to another search consultant with more experience in my field, but in many cases, if the jobhunter does not meet the correct search consultant initially, then a lot of time can be lost. And sometimes you never meet the right search consultant for your skill set."

CASE STUDY

EDS wants 'added value'

Information technology services company EDS operates in 55 companies, employing more than 130,000 people globally, including 17,000 in the UK. In the course of a year, it used search consultants to recruit for between 50 and 60 roles, focusing their efforts as part of a broader recruitment strategy on high-end or difficult-to-fill senior management and technical vacancies.

The company's David Mason says that while many organisations are now more knowledgeable about recruitment and selection – at least in part because they have brought recruitment industry expertise in-house – there remains a place for consultants. The sheer time, effort and knowledge involved in effective headhunting can make this an area that justifies the use of expensive external expertise.

He says: "Search consultants and the whole idea of search is often a numbers game, so what they may or may not tell you is that to find one candidate, then they need to present between three and five candidates. To get to that shortlist, they need to interview about 15 people. And to find those 15 people, they need to telephone and have a general conversation with between 70 and 100 people. That is the sort of back-end work that needs to be going on."

Not all vacancies are suitable ground for headhunters. "You have to clearly define to yourself what it is you're looking for," says David Mason. "That's the first step. It sounds very, very obvious, but thinking about what you're going into the market to find will really help to decide what kind of recruitment methodology you use."

He gives the example of looking for a computer programme developer. Using search consultants would not be a very effective way of recruiting for such a position because there is a very diffused target market. He says: "Search tends to work best when you've got a well-defined target group to contact and it's more effective for search consultants to go in and perform their role."

Search consultants can also provide a comfort zone for employers. Few personnel departments would want to be involved in the process of gathering commercially sensitive information from competitors and poaching key members of their staff. "Search consultants add value to the recruitment process through their understanding of the market place, knowing where to go and look, but also understanding the different market variables and how people are approached in that market," says David Mason.

But how do you decide on a search consultant? EDS uses difference consultants for different roles. "A lot of it comes down to track record on what they've delivered before or having a personal knowledge of their capabilities. One of the most important elements of the whole search consultancy is down to how good an individual consultant is," says David Mason. "While some companies are trying to get a quality standard attached to the work they do, the industry as a whole is only as good or professional as the weakest individual consultant."

Even with the right consultant in place, he warns, there can be a view that they are not adding value within the recruitment process. Consultants themselves have to take a long hard view at where they add value, he adds. "We don't just want to see someone delivering 'bodies' to us. We want them to play a role in the recruitment fundamentals, like playing a role in the selection of staff, preparing job descriptions, key elements of the process that can go wrong."

CASE STUDY

Lewisham council focuses on senior roles

London Borough of Lewisham uses search consultants only to recruit into director and other senior posts. "We started using search consultants around 10 years ago and we use them for high-profile, higher-paid senior positions. We also have problems filling some lower-level jobs, but search consultants won't get involved in recruiting for a job with a salary below £35,000 or £40,000," says Tim Anderson, a strategic personnel adviser in the borough.

Lewisham adopts an approach favoured by many employers. It uses headhunters to complement its recruitment advertising, rather than replace it with a completely informal approach.

Tim Anderson says there are a number of reasons why Lewisham uses search consultants in the way that it does: "One is that we want to guarantee that we've trawled the market completely for the best possible people. It's also important PR that we're prepared to do creative advertising for these posts as well as invest significant resources using search consultants. It helps the image of the organisation. We have an excellent reputation within local government, and the search consultants are building on this so they can sell not only the job, but the organisation as well."

He goes on to say: "It means that we can attract those people who see the adverts, but also search consultants can sweep up others who may not normally apply but through contact with search consultants may be persuaded. It's really a two-pronged approach, it helps attract those who are looking and unearths those who need persuading."

Tim Anderson warns that to get the best value out of recruitment consultants, it is important to plan ahead - a luxury not always affordable when filling vacancies. "I think there is a role for search consultants. The main issues for me are about whether or not we should use search automatically for senior posts. Sometimes, the recruitment timescales do not allow time to consider whether search would add value and can lead to engagement without full consideration of all the options," he says.

Chapter 6
Employee referral payments

Employers have always relied on word of mouth to fill vacancies. But as skills shortages have begun to bite, many employers have sought to systematise their use of informal recruitment by introducing bonuses, known as bounty or referral payments, for existing employees who put forward candidates who make successful recruits.

In this chapter we look at the factors that make a good scheme work, and the potential problems that might arise, focusing on the experience of a wide range of employers, among them: coffee shop chain Pret A Manger, mobile phone manufacturer Nokia, computer manufacturer Hewlett-Packard, insurance company Scottish Equitable and the Royal Surrey Hospital.

THE CASE FOR BOUNTY PAYMENTS

- They produce high-quality candidates because employees are usually careful only to recommend people they think will be suitable for the organisation, so that they act as a first-line filter for applications.

- They help organisations maintain links to reliable sources of suitable skills. At Nokia, for instance, engineering and technical support staff who have an armed forces background may alert former colleagues as they leave the services.

- They breed a culture where everyone is responsible for recruitment.

THE CASE AGAINST BOUNTY PAYMENTS

- When publicity, HR time and the cost of the bonuses are factored in, they are no cheaper than other methods of recruitment.

- Where the jobs on offer are not highly-skilled ones, the prospect of a cash payment can encourage over-enthusiasm on the part of a few employees.

- Schemes need to be focused, perhaps stressing minimum skill requirements, or they can result in an overwhelming response from largely unqualified candidates.

- Competition with rival companies could lead to spiralling bonus payments.

- Over-reliance on referral carries the risk of "cloning" the existing workforce, bringing in more and more of the same type of recruit.

HOW TO MAKE A BOUNTY SCHEME WORK

Keep it simple

Most referral schemes are generally not constrained by a long list of rules and caveats. One common to most schemes, however, is that the person referred must work for a qualifying period before the bounty payment is made. Some organisations, such as Pret A Manger, set this period at three months; others, including Royal Surrey Hospital, specify a more cautious six months. Hewlett-Packard is unusual in making the payment immediately upon recruitment.

Another restriction employed by some organisations excludes senior members of staff from an entitlement to referral payments. Many HR managers question whether managers should receive an extra reward for recommending suitable applicants, especially when recruiting for their own team, as this could be seen as part of their normal duties. Nokia typically excludes both managers and HR staff from referral payments.

Stay in touch

Although referral schemes are cheap and reliable, they can create extra work for HR staff. Apart from the need to communicate the scheme, most organisations guarantee employees referring friends or family an acknowledgement of the referral; this is no small commitment if the arrangement generates hundreds of leads each month.

Hewlett-Packard's Julia Colin notes that the easiest way to respond would be by a generic "thank you" email. "But we have found the more human the interface, the better it works," she says. Employees that make a referral at Hewlett-Packard receive a personal phone call or email.

Feedback to employees on their referrals is an important means of maintaining enthusiasm. Steve Carpenter, HR manager at Pret A Manger, notes that it is not always a simple matter and requires a sense of diplomacy. "You have to be quite careful about how you communicate to people why you didn't take up their recommendation of a friend or family member," he points out.

The employers that we contacted all emphasised the importance of good internal publicity to the continued success of their schemes. Most said they brief all new employees about their referral programmes as part of induction. Workplace posters and leaflets, email reminders and notices published in in-house magazines are also used.

Scottish Equitable reminds employees about its Friends and Family programme via line management briefings, while train operator Connex targeted its first referral campaign with direct mailshots to employees' homes. Nokia is also considering the use of direct marketing to bolster employee awareness of its scheme.

HOW MUCH SHOULD YOU PAY?

A recruiter looking for a benchmark for bounty payments will find it difficult to pin down a going rate. Levels vary widely across employment sectors and job types, reflecting the scarcity of skills and their relative value to the organisations concerned. Among those with established bounty payment programmes:

- Pret A Manger offers a modest £50 per successful referral – though this rises to £2,000 for referrals to management jobs. The company estimates that around 10% of its 2,000 recruits in one year came through its bounty scheme.

- The Royal Surrey Hospital in Guildford normally pays £250.

- The UK arm of mobile phone manufacturer Nokia operates a scale of payments according to the scarcity of the skills sought.

As employers' needs change, however, so do bounty schemes. Computer giant Hewlett-Packard used a sliding scale of £250 to £5,000, but is revamping its scheme and replacing the range with a set payment of £2,000 for most jobs. "The company wants a simple global system, and we were asked at country level to come up with a workable sum that would work budgetwise and be attractive," explains Julia Colin of the company's HR department.

In the USA last year, internet systems supplier Nortel Networks supplemented its $2,000 (£1,350) bounty for successful referrals with the promise of entry to a draw with a prize fund of $1 million (£680,540), from which individuals could win up to $100,000 (£68,038) each. Level3 is also looking into the possibility of a lottery for employees making referrals, in addition to its existing payments.

But if such emphasis on payments and prizes seems to indicate that referral schemes have to appeal to employees' self-interest to succeed, the "Friends and Family" scheme operated by insurer Scottish Equitable suggests otherwise. Recruitment Manager Carole Lamond says the programme works well enough without bounty payments. "That's the kind of culture we have here," she explains. "We have a good community atmosphere, and we believe it is a good place to work and we reward people well."

CASE STUDY

Royal Surrey County Hospital finds publicity works

The experience of Royal Surrey Hospital suggests that a bounty scheme can succeed even if it fails to produce many recommendations, provided it receives the right exposure.

The hospital has run a "Recruit a friend" scheme for the past two-and-a-half years, paying a bonus of £250 for successful referrals for hard-to-fill posts. Recruitment problems are especially acute for the lower-skilled jobs, according to personnel adviser Ros Walker. "The cost of living in Guildford is the same as in London, but we do not get the additional allowances," she explains.

One summer recently, the shortage of nurses in the hospital's intensive care unit was so desperate - it had caused several beds to be closed - that the personnel staff raised the bounty for referrals in that job group to £1,000.

In the narrow sense, the initiative was not a success, producing only one successful referral. However, the size of the payment caused it to be picked up by the local and national press. This media interest in turn led to a raft of applications from suitably-trained nurses.

Ros Walker says the hospital now has its full complement of ICU nurses, the beds have been reopened and several applicants who did not have appropriate experience are undergoing intensive care training to buttress the unit against any future skills shortages.

She warns that bounty payments are not without their problems. At the low skill end there may be people who are willing to exploit the system. In some cases, she says it is obvious that members of staff in domestic posts will serve out the six months necessary to qualify their friend for their £250 referral payment and then leave. Worse than this, in a few cases such people will reapply after a short interval using a recommendation from the same friend in the hope of a second payment. "We only pay out once," she notes firmly.

Chapter 7
Effective application forms

Application forms are an integral part of the selection process – second only to interviews as the most favoured selection tool. But while they are widely used in the public sector and in larger organisations, many smaller, private sector employers prefer to rely CVs instead. In this chapter we compare the strengths of the two approaches and look at ways to make application forms work more effectively.

THE CASE FOR APPLICATION FORMS

- They set a level playing field for all applicants.

- As all applicants will have addressed the same issues, they provide employers with a standard set of starting points for subsequent interviews.

- Candidates for lower level jobs may be able to complete an application form but lack the experience to compile a CV.

THE CASE AGAINST APPLICATION FORMS

- They may constrain a good candidate's ability to sell themselves by restricting the range of possible responses.

- A poorly designed form or one which asks irrelevant questions reflects badly on the organisation.

- Unless properly tailored to the vacancy they run the risk of breaching data protection laws.

APPLICATION FORMS VERSUS CVs

The Chartered Institute of Personnel and Development[1] says that CVs are more regularly used for managerial and professional posts than for lower-level vacancies. That study, and research conducted by IRS[2], also found that smaller employers, possibly with fewer resources at their disposal, tend to favour more informal recruitment and selection procedures and are more prepared to accept CVs or a mixture of CVs and application forms.

Brighton and Hove Council currently accepts only application forms for its vacancies, but is considering the possibility of also accepting CVs in certain circumstances. Vanda

Duncliffe, senior HR officer with the council, explains: "There is a view that permitting CV applications in some cases would open up the recruitment process to members of the community who may find it difficult to complete the standard form."

For employers, the main benefit of the application form is that it sets a level playing field: all applicants are required to answer the same questions in the same way, which should aid objectivity. But this could also be a drawback if the format, with defined space for each response, is too restrictive and does not provide sufficient opportunities for candidates to demonstrate their skills and abilities.

A frequently cited benefit of the CV is the freedom it provides "to sell yourself". But this too presents problems. A CV will not be as focused as an application form, which can make it more difficult to judge the information provided. In turn, this can make shortlisting more onerous and possibly less reliable.

MAKING THE MOST OF APPLICATION FORMS

Think about what your form is for

Application forms are generally the first stage of the selection process, and the information they provide – such as personal details, educational background and work experience – is used to filter applicants on to a shortlist for interview. The form's contents can then be used as a point of reference by interviewers, prompting follow-up questions and indicating areas that may need clarification.

Application forms are also a good PR tool. Paperwork distributed as part of the recruitment process can help to promote the image of the employing organisation – provided it has been well designed. Some organisations send out "application packs" to prospective candidates, enclosing relevant and attractive literature that boost the employer's profile.

Tailor your application forms

One solution to the problem of rigidity of application forms is to tailor the form to specific vacancies. Forms designed with a core set of questions, supplemented by focused questions for each vacancy or group of vacancies, can help ensure a balance between consistency and flexibility. Given that the most effective application forms are those that pay close attention to the person specification and core competencies required for the post, making them more specific to the individual post also makes them a more useful tool.

With the software available on a typical office computer, the design of such forms need not be laborious or costly. Application forms are a relatively inexpensive selection tool compared with, for example, the cost of running assessment centres.

There is now another compelling reason for not using a standard application form across all vacancies. The Employment Practices data protection code[3] - which gives guidance on how the Data Protection Act 1998 should be interpreted - says information should be collected only when it is needed for selection. This casts serious doubt on the use of standard forms because they invariably request information that is not specifically relevant to all vacancies. The information requested on a job application form must not be "excessive, irrelevant or inadequate".

Going online

While the use of the internet in recruitment is patchy, there is plenty of evidence to show that it is becoming more common. The IRS study mentioned above showed that 60% of employers involved in electronic recruitment accept CVs emailed to them, while 33% accept completed application forms via email. But the obvious advantages of using electronic forms of recruitment, such as speed and the ability to cast a much wider recruitment net, have to be balanced against possible pitfalls. The workload can increase, for instance, if applications and email communications are printed off and handled in the traditional, paper-based way.

There is also a possibility that an unmanageable number of applications will be generated. Tesco Pharmacy, for example, currently accepts applications via CV for its pharmacist posts electronically, but believes that developing an online application form is a priority for the future. As Carol Trower, Tesco Pharmacy's recruitment and training manager, explains: "Our website generates a lot of interest, but because would-be candidates can currently submit only a CV, a high proportion of applications do not meet the necessary criteria." She believes that an application form could have a screening facility, which would specify the necessary pharmacy qualifications and filter out unsuitable applications.

What doesn't work?

Very little thought is often paid to the design of application forms – even though a poorly designed form can act as negative marketing for the organisation or deter people from completing them. Research for the Society of Personnel Officers in Local Government also found that long application forms put candidates off[4].

There are other possible pitfalls. For example, it is common practice for application forms to distinguish between "current" and "previous" employment. This could be a disadvantage to a candidate who is not currently in full-time employment. Similarly, the practice could discourage someone from applying if they have concerns about the length of time they have been in their current position. Designing an application form so as to gather information on the skills and attributes of the candidate that are relevant to the job is one way of addressing the above issues.

A NOTE ABOUT THE LAW

Equal opportunities

It is unlawful to discriminate on the grounds of disability, race and sex but, by December 2006, age discrimination will also be prohibited by law under article 13 of the EU Employment Directive. Discrimination on the grounds of religion and sexual orientation will also be banned.

As a first step towards outlawing age discrimination, the government has introduced a Code of Practice[5] that includes advice on reducing the risk of discrimination when designing application forms. It recommends that those involved in the selection process should not to see candidates' unnecessary personal details. For monitoring purposes, personal details should be separated and re-introduced at the end of the recruitment process. The CIPD also recommends that information collected for equal opportunities monitoring should be kept separate from information on which selection decisions are based, and be used only for monitoring purposes.

Monitoring

Monitoring recruitment on the basis of race and gender has been an integral part of many organisations' equal opportunities policies since the mid-1980s. As well as providing a possible defence against claims of unlawful discrimination, employers are increasingly adopting policies to encourage diversity in their employment practices. Equality agencies have long advocated monitoring the demographics of applicants so as to analyse the profile of the workforce. This is a process that can offer evidence that organisations are effective in attracting applications from different sections of the community.

Also, recording the source of job applications can help an organisation target future advertising to attract underrepresented groups. The Race Relations (Amendment) Act 2000 places a legal duty on public sector organisations to promote equality of opportunity and publish the results of their ethnic monitoring exercises.

With the advent of the Disability Discrimination Act 1995 (DDA), asking a question relating to a candidate's disability on application forms has become more prevalent. Asking job applicants if they have a disability helps organisations to comply with the DDA requirement to make reasonable adjustments. If an individual indicates that they have a disability, then necessary arrangements or adjustments can be made from the outset, usually starting with the interview. The DDA employment Code of Practice[6] provides comprehensive advice on the treatment of disabled people in the recruitment process.

Data Protection Act

The Data Protection Act 1998 came into force in March 2000. It applies to manual as well as computerised records. In March 2002, the Information Commissioner began issuing a four-part Employment practices data protection code. Data protection law has far-reaching implications for the employment relationship, not least in the collection of information for monitoring purposes.

The code specifies that if sensitive information is collected, such as that relating to racial or ethnic origin, political opinions or sexual life, at least one "sensitive data condition" must be satisfied. The specific circumstances in which such data can be obtained are spelt out and include reasons such as: a legal obligation in connection with employment; where the individual in question has given explicit consent; or as part of equal opportunities monitoring.

The code sets out these further benchmarks with reference to job applications:

- "state, on any application form, to whom the information is being provided and how it will be used if this is not self-evident;

- only seek personal data that are relevant to the recruitment decision being made;

- only request information about an applicant's criminal convictions if that information can be justified in terms of the role offered. If this information is justified, make it clear that spent convictions do not have to be declared, unless the job being filled is covered by the Exceptions Order to the Rehabilitation of Offenders Act 1974;

- explain any checks that might be undertaken to verify the information provided in the application form including the nature of additional sources from which information may be gathered; and

- provide a secure method for sending applications."

There are also clear guidelines on retaining recruitment records, such as the need to establish and adhere to retention periods for such documents, which are based on a business need. Employers should also consider carefully what information should be transferred to an employee's employment record and should delete data relating to ongoing employment. If information about unsuccessful candidates is to be retained for future vacancies, they should be informed and be given the opportunity to have their details removed from the file.

CASE STUDY

Peugeot focuses on design and content

Coventry-based carmaker Peugeot changed the design and content of its application forms to improve the reliability of its shortlisting process, and to cut down the number of people taken forward in the selection process. The application form for one group of workers now includes questions relating to applicants' experience of shiftworking, for example, and the equal opportunities section has been expanded.

The old application form, which had remained unchanged for a number of years, did not provide Peugeot with enough information to screen out inappropriate candidates. A company spokesperson says the new forms have proved successful, helping the company to identify applicants who do not meet its requirements but who may have been invited for production-line tests and interview under the previous system.

Sources

1. Recruitment and retention 2002, Chartered Institute of Personnel and Development, May 2002, www.cipd.co.uk.

2. "Applying the changes", *IRS Employment Review* 761, October 2002.

3. Employment practices data protection code, www.dataprotection.gov.uk.

4. The mirror image, Society of Personnel Officers in Local Government, www.socpo.org.uk.

5. Code of Practice on age diversity, www.agepositive.gov.uk.

6. Code of Practice for the elimination of discrimination in the field of employment against disabled persons or persons who have had a disability, www.drc-gb.org.

Chapter 8
Effective interviews

Interviews are by some way the most popular selection tool, and three out of four employers who use interviews at all do so for every single vacancy. However, most employers no longer believe that interviews alone are the best way to appoint someone to a job, and many prefer to think about how an interview will fit into their overall selection procedure.

This chapter looks at the different approaches to interviews, looks at recent trends among employers and offers guidance on running a successful interview process. In doing so it draws on the views of 60 employers whose approach to interviewing was studied by IRS[1].

THE CASE FOR INTERVIEWS

- Few other selection methods allow such an insight into the candidates.

- A face-to-face meeting offers both employer and potential employee to check detailed information, get a feel for each other and start to negotiate the employment contract.

- They are a useful way of "selling" the job and the employer to potential recruits.

THE CASE AGAINST INTERVIEWS

- A short face-to-face meeting may favour candidates who are plausible over those who are capable.

- Irrelevant detail such as a candidate's appearance or personal dislike on the part of the selector may influence the outcome.

- There is a temptation to rely on the interview alone rather than to see it as one of a range of tools.

CHOOSING THE RIGHT KIND OF INTERVIEW

Choosing the right interview is a matter of cost and format. The approach taken has to meet the needs of the organisation, reflect the importance of the job to be filled, and be appropriate to the role it has to fill in the overall selection process – as an initial screening tool, or a final stage before the appointment is made.

The checklist below looks at the strengths and weaknesses of some of the different formats available. But there are also different approaches that can be taken. These are explored here.

Structured interviews

A structured interview has a format that is planned in advance. Every section and question has been developed and placed in an order to draw out information that is relevant to the job.

However, structured interviews need not determine the entire content and sequence of the process. They can also allow the opportunity for certain issues flagged up during the conversation to be probed and explored in more detail.

The IRS study mentioned above found that nearly nine out of 10 employers prefer this approach. And while it remains more commonly used to fill management jobs, it is popular with most employers across the whole range of posts.

Situational interviews

Situational interviews give candidates the opportunity to display their competence and abilities even if they do not possess specific experience. By using predetermined questions and situations – ideally drawn from a scenario related to the vacancy – candidates can give practical examples of how they would cope. This type of interview involves asking questions such as "What would you do if …" or "What did you do when …".

Nine out of 10 employers sometimes use this approach, but it appears to be used more selectively than structured interviews. The IRS study found that less than two-thirds of employers use "what if" questions when selecting for manual positions, but more than four in five use them for selecting individuals for professional or managerial roles.

However, structured and situational formats are probably most effective when used together. Our research showed that nearly nine out of 10 respondents use both structured and situational methods to interview candidates. Reasons they gave for this include:

- "it slightly improves an unreliable selection method";

- "it gives candidates the opportunity to relate what they know and how they would apply it";

- "it gives us greater insight into the candidates"; and

- "ensuring we get the same information from each candidate".

Behavioural event interviews

The behaviourally-based interview – or Patterned Behavioural Description Interview – is a relatively new way of focusing the questions in an interview. The behaviour-based interview concentrates exclusively on drawing information on actual past experience rather than hypothetical situations. This type of questioning is often used in competency-based interviews.

This highly-structured interview takes much time and effort to develop. The construction of interview schedules requires analysing the job using the critical incident technique, a method where incidents critical to the success or otherwise of the job are collected through a series of interviews with job experts and grouped into dimensions such as technical skills, motivation etc, which represent the major characteristics of the job.

Another group of experts is then handed the set of critical incidents and is asked to identify particular incidents that it feels represent the dimensions. These are then prepared as questions – typically between 10 and 20 – for use in the interview.

Benchmark answers are developed for each of the questions by the job experts and a scale is prepared to score the interviewees' responses. The end result is a benchmark answer and examples of good, average and poor replies, which act as a guide for the interviewer and can help create a framework for standardised assessment.

The reasons that behavioural event interviews seem to produce better results than conventional approaches may lie in the fact that the content of the interview becomes firmly focused on job-relevant topics and is standardised so that all interviewees are questioned according to a common strategy.

RUNNING SUCCESSFUL INTERVIEWS

How many interviews?

There are no hard-and-fast rules about the number of interviews that should be conducted, and this is possibly one of those areas where it really is the quality of the information you receive that is important rather than the number of attempts you make to obtain it. One good interview will be more effective and add more to the selection procedure that several unfocused, rambling dialogues.

However, it has become more common for more than one interview to be held, perhaps with the initial interview acting as a screening process conducted by the personnel department rather than by those who will be directly involved with the individual. It also depends on the nature and seniority of the position. Nine in 10 employers in our research hold more than one interview as part of their selection procedure.

In contrast, some employers are moving to simplify interview stages. This may be due to the changes within the personnel role over the past decade. Line managers with direct responsibility for the applicant are now becoming more active in the recruitment and selection process, and as a result may be conducting the interview themselves. Or it may be due to the realisation that interviews, while influential, play just one part in the overall selection process.

How many interviewers?

Selection interviews involving a single interviewer raise many difficult issues, and these are dealt with in the checklist below that looks at interview formats. IRS research shows that employers recognise the dangers of conducting interviews with just one interviewer present. Almost half of the interview situations in our research were conducted by two interviewers. The highest number of interviewers feature in the selection of professionals and managers where usually more than three interviewers are involved.

It has been suggested that three interviewers is the ideal number, and should include the person to whom the candidate will report. It is this person who should also make the final selection decision, on the advice of the others. It is felt that if only two people are involved in the final interview stage, it might prove difficult to reach agreement, but this should be made easier with a third person. Any more than three is felt to be intimidating for the candidate, but this may differ depending on the level of the post concerned.

Getting it right

By the time the interview takes place, both the interviewer and interviewees will have made a substantial investment in the process, and this should be recognised. The interview as a tool to provide favourable impressions of the organisation should not be underestimated. Also, the interviewer must try to impart a positive yet realistic picture of an organisation that an individual would wish to work for.

One of the keys to maximising the effectiveness of the interview process depends on ensuring those involved in the interview process have been properly trained in both delivering the questions and interpreting the answers.

Setting the scene

It is important to create a controlled environment in which to conduct the interview. This is widely recognised as an important foundation for an effective interviewing process, and involves such issues as ensuring a temperate climate in a room and preventing disturbances, unless in the case of an emergency.

Those conducting the interview need to think about how much time will be spent putting the interviewee at ease, perhaps asking about the journey to the interview or making banal comments on the weather. This is an important part of the interview as it allows the interviewee the opportunity to become acclimatised to the situation and feel more at ease. They will then have the chance of presenting themselves in the best possible way during the main part of the interview. If a panel or group interview is taking place, then it is important that this part of the process has been discussed and agreed between the interviewers beforehand.

It is also useful to tell the candidate what form the interview will take and what, if anything, will happen directly afterwards – there may be a further assessment taking place or interviewees may have to wait to be given feedback. By ensuring the candidate is as comfortable and as informed as possible, the interviewer is preparing the ground for an effective interview.

It is now that the dedicated interviewing skills come into play – effective questioning, active listening, productive feedback and summarising.

Reducing unconscious bias

Interviewers should seek to create an environment where only predetermined, objective selection criteria form the basis for the decision-making process. This rarely if ever occurs, as subjective elements will always be present, but it is vital that every effort is made.

We make decisions and form impressions of people based on a personal system of beliefs that we have developed through our lifetime. It is this system that allows us to rationalise the past, understand the present and make predictions for the future. But this process also allows an interviewer to stereotype an individual, resulting in a positive or negative effect on their perception or decision about the individual.

It is important to recognise this and deal with it. Whether conscious or subconscious, these beliefs or impressions play a role in how people prepare for situations, how they act and react, and how they seek to perform a role so as to be judged or perceived in a certain way. Such developed beliefs also play a role in the way decisions are made, consciously or not[2].

Other biases or errors that can enter into the selection process include the "halo effect" and – from the other end of the scale – the "satan effect". Both arise as a result of generalisations and oversimplifications, and usually take the form of:

- something that comes to the attention of the interviewer concerning the candidate that puts them in a good light, which will then be taken by the interviewer as a sample of their total ability (halo effect);

- a poor opinion of some aspect of the interviewee's past experience, which may be transferred as a poor opinion about the individual, often subconsciously (the satan effect).

Body language

The issue of body language – including paraverbal behaviour (tone of voice and hesitations in speech) and non-verbal behaviour, such as posture and gesticulation – and the impact it has on the overall selection decision continues to generate much discussion and interest. This subject has something akin to a folklore tradition with various figures and percentages making regular appearances at training days, management programmes or interview preparation days.

Interviewers who become aware of their judgment being affected by "a gut reaction" or "instinct" should not ignore such feelings - but try to back up their feelings through probing questions or seeking clarification. This is something that can also be addressed at the reference gathering stage. Intuition is a very powerful personal tool and, all other things being equal, there is a strong case for it being taken into account.

Dress sense

The issue of presentation in an interview and the feelings it arouses in the interviewer need to be treated most carefully. Smart dress is no longer required in many workplaces and, indeed, some organisations encourage employees to express themselves and their creativity through their wardrobe. It is important to put appearance or dress sense into the context of the vacancy being filled.

Role of memory

Memory is also subjective and unreliable and can be distorted for a number of reasons. It has been recognised that those people we meet first and last are better remembered that those who are encountered in the middle of a sequence. It is also the case that those who distinguish themselves in some way, either through an outstanding feature or some act out of the ordinary, are remembered more easily than others. However, this does not mean that a decision will favour those who stood out or are more easily remembered – it may have the opposite effect.

EFFECTIVE INTERVIEW SKILLS

Questioning

The most effective types of questions are those that encourage the candidate to open up and respond at length. This then facilitates two-way dialogue. Open-ended questions – prefixed by "how", "what", or "why" – encourage the employee to think carefully without being prompted by the content or phrasing of the question.

It is useful to begin the interview with questions that are positive and encourage the candidate to talk about themselves. Also, questions that do not require too much thought initially are useful so that the candidate will have an opportunity to begin to feel comfortable in the surroundings, without immediately feeling under pressure.

More complex questions should be introduced in the middle of the interview and final questions should seek to clarify any areas that were raised during the interview. Queries should be resolved prior to the close of interview so that assessment of the candidate can be properly completed.

Questioning techniques that should be avoided include closed questions which elicit only a "yes" or "no" response and do not encourage further discussion. However, they do have a role in clarifying particular points. Examples of such a question include:

- "Are you ready to start straight away?"

- "Do you like working with people?" and

- "Are you happy working with people?"

Questions that prompt or lead candidates should be avoided. Such questions normally give strong indications of what the required answer should be. These include questions like:

- "You would be happy to do that, wouldn't you?" and

- "That would be the wrong thing to do, wouldn't it?"

It is difficult for the interviewee to answer a question that addresses two issues or covers more than one topic. In this situation, the interviewee will probably choose to answer the last question or the easiest one. An example of this type of question would be:

CHECKLIST

How to run an effective interview

Before the interview

- Ensure you have an up-to-date job description for the post and are familiar with it. Think about others who work in that environment and their particular skills sets.

- An up-to-date person specification will be needed, again ensure you are familiar with its contents.

- Be conversant with the conditions of employment for the role.

- Be aware of any training and development available for this particular role and throughout the organisation in general.

- Spend time getting to know the candidates' application forms or CVs, and make a note of any areas you will want to probe or clarify.

- Ensure there is a suitable interviewing room available and make every effort to ensure you will not be disturbed.

- Decide on your method of recording your notes from the interview, preferably using an interview assessment form.

- If relevant, meet your co-interviewers to discuss format and plan strategy.

During the interview

- Introduce yourself and your colleagues (if present) and welcome the candidate.

- Spend some time initially putting the candidate at his or her ease.

- Work to your schedule, but do not be afraid to probe or seek clarification where necessary.

- Describe the role and what will be involved on a day-to-day basis.

- Avoid making any assumptions.

- Be aware of personal bias, asking secondary questions if necessary.

- Keep in mind the job and person specification at all times.

- Avoid arguing or giving your opinion but instead listen to and question the interviewee on his or her opinions.

- Make brief notes throughout.

- Listen actively, looking for reasons and feelings behind the facts.

- Invite questions.

- Describe the next steps.

After the interview

- Do not rush into a decision directly after the interview but allow yourself time to reflect objectively at a later stage.

- Discuss in detail the job specification and the person specification with your co-interviewers and how the candidate did or did not meet the criteria.

- Evaluate your person specification and application form.

- "How did you enjoy that experience, was it good, or would you have preferred to do something else, did your colleagues think it was a good idea?"

The last stage of the interview should provide the candidate with the opportunity to ask questions about the organisation or the job or, indeed, how to claim their travel expenses.

Active listening

People think faster than they speak, and this skill can be used effectively in an interview situation as it allows the interviewer to concentrate on what is being said and try to pick up the underlying message. Active listening allows the interviewer to manage the interview situation effectively without unnecessary repetition or dwelling too long on one subject. A good active listener will also help to make the interviewee feel comfortable and believe what he or she is saying is something of worth.

To ensure constructive active listening, avoid:

- tuning out of the conversation when nothing interesting appears to be forthcoming;

- interrupting or guessing the end of a sentence; and

- losing concentration and becoming easily distracted by outside or peripheral "noise".

Feedback and summarising

Body language plays an important role in letting the interviewee know that their message is getting through and that the interviewer is listening and absorbing what is being said. Nodding of the head to indicate agreement, leaning forward to indicate interest in what is being said, smiling to encourage more information and make the candidate feel comfortable – each of these things can encourage the candidate to give more information or become more comfortable so the quality of the information is improved.

Positive feedback also encourages the candidate to feel good and offer more information. Summarising what the candidate has said is one way of offering feedback. It is also effective to reflect the feelings that the candidate has been expressing as well as the facts. This has the extra advantage of giving the interviewee the opportunity to clarify the statement if it has been misinterpreted.

CHECKLIST

Interview formats at a glance

One-to-one interviews

One of the few advantages of a one-to-one interview, in which the selector meets the candidate alone, is the casual atmosphere that can be created. Candidates may be much more at ease if there is only one interviewer and thus more open.

However, time constraints often create a situation where one-to-one interviews become necessary. It is very time consuming for more than one individual to be present at each interview stage, particularly if selection is still at the initial stages.

The main problem with this approach is that a lone interviewer will find it harder to concentrate on remembering fully what the candidate has said while also thinking ahead to consider points to probe. Another disadvantage is that the interviewer is open to all the biases and errors of perception. A lone interviewer does not have the advantage of checking perceptions or assumptions with another interviewer.

The interviewer in this type of situation is also left open to accusations of malpractice. The interviewer is in an extremely vulnerable position without someone else being present, and this isolation will make it difficult to rebut allegations made by a disgruntled candidate. Finally, the candidate can find themselves exposed to illegal discrimination and malpractice.

One way to ensure as many pitfalls as possible are avoided is by asking each candidate the same set of pre-prepared questions.

Informal interviews

Informal interviews adopt an unstructured format and, when part of a broader selection process, tend to take place between the candidate and two or more interviewers who then go on to relay their impressions to the final interview panel or appointment board. The main is that it allows topics to be explored and a two-way dialogue to be developed. However, this can be confusing for the candidate and those involved in the selection process. The lack of structure can mean that other factors – such as group dynamics – come into play.

This type of interview can be advantageous for the candidate as it can give them a clear picture of the organisation's culture and help them decide whether they are likely to fit in.

Panel interviews

This method uses two or more interviewers, but is distinct from a *two-person* interview. In this arrangement, there may be a clear division of labour with different interviewers exploring different aspects of the candidate's suitability. Studies show that unstructured board interviews produce higher levels of validity than unstructured individual interviews.

Good planning and preparation to ensure a consistent approach to interviewing based on the prepared person and job specifications is essential. It is also important that the mix of people who are put together to conduct the interviews is such that the dynamics of the group adds something constructive to the process.

Telephone interviewing

Given the rise of telecommunications and the introduction of more distance-based communication, it is perhaps unsurprising that telephone interviewing has become increasingly common. Organisations are now using the telephone to conduct initial screening interviews, and usage may grow further in the future. This subject is dealt with in more depth in Chapter 9.

Sources

1. "The interview: its role in selection", *Employee Development Bulletin* 122, February 2000; "The business of selection: an IRS survey", *Employee Development Bulletin* 117, September 1999.

2. *Successful recruitment and selection: a practical guide for managers*, Margaret Dale, Kogan Page, pp. 162–165, 1995.

Chapter 9
Telephone interviewing

A small but growing number of organisations make use of telephone screening – some as part of their shortlisting process, others for specific jobs where telephone skills form a key part of the work, such as in call centres. This chapter looks in detail at the experience of three companies that have used this novel approach: energy and home services company Centrica, IT services provider EDS and financial services company Scottish Equitable, each of whom was driven by different reasons to adopt it. It also reports on the approach of companies as diverse as DIY retailer B&Q and the Royal Bank of Scotland.

THE CASE FOR TELEPHONE INTERVIEWS

- They are cost-effective and efficient, helping to screen out unsuitable candidates at a very early stage, and may be the only practical solution when a company is recruiting internationally.

- They reduce distractions based on the applicant's appearance and cuts down the danger of discrimination on grounds of age, race and disability.

- They enable employers to get a good idea of a candidates' competence where telephone manner is a central part of the job.

THE CASE AGAINST TELEPHONE INTERVIEWS

- They require careful planning, with proper training offered to interviewers and a well-structured interview format

- They may deter good applicants who regard a telephone interview as a poor substitute for personal contact and believe it represents a lack of commitment on the employer's part.

- They have hidden costs and employers may need to devote considerable resources to making contact with some candidates.

WHY EMPLOYERS USE THIS APPROACH

Figures from the Chartered Institute of Personnel and Development[1] show that 17% of UK employers currently use this telephone interviews – most commonly in the services industries in the private sector, where more than a quarter (27%) do so, compared with around one in 10 manufacturers (10.6%) and slightly fewer (9.2%) in the public sector. But so far employer practice has been running ahead of the theory, with little research evidence to show whether telephone interviewing helps employers select the right candidates, and how it compares to other approaches.

Many employers that have adopted telephone interviewing do so to keep costs down. The trend towards more efficient recruitment has been partly driven by the need to cut back on organisational costs and focus on delivery, and partly by the increasingly global approach of many employers, with geographically dispersed workforces and international recruitment now more common.

Many organisations, particularly larger ones, also look for diversity in their workforce, which means they want to reduce irrelevant barriers to employment, and be able to interview people from a wider geographical area. For international candidates telephone interviewing, at least initially, is often the only practical option. It both reduces travel costs and speeds up the recruitment process.

A third factor driving companies towards telephone interviewing is recruitment outsourcing. To give one example, Royal Bank of Scotland (RBS) contracted out its graduate recruitment programme to PSL in 2001. The aim, according to Fiona Brazil, manager for graduate resourcing at RBS, was "to take away our administration" to fit in with the company's view of personnel specialists as consultants. All applicants are screened online before taking part in a telephone interview.

HOW TELEPHONE INTERVIEWS HELP

There are good practical reasons for using telephone interviews. It is as easy to run through a structured interview over the telephone as it is face to face. There are fewer distractions and a greater focus on the task. In theory, there is less opportunity to discriminate on the grounds of race, disability, age or other factors.

Telephone interviews are, for example, a key component of superstore B&Q's centralised phone-in Recruitment Response Centre at Tannochside, Glasgow, operated through Port@l. When applicants call Tannochside, their full details are entered into the centre's database and they are given their own PIN and details of a freephone contact number. Because B&Q wants to be non-discriminatory, no personal details are discussed in the follow-up telephone interview. Questions are aimed only at measuring whether or not the candidate is likely to fit into the company culture and enjoy working there.

Once through this "front-gate" process, candidates' applications are viewed by the local stores and matched with vacancy criteria. Tannochside now handles all the company's shopfloor staffing requirements for the UK and Dublin. In one year alone the company recruited more than 6,000 staff through the centre.

PROBLEMS YOU MAY ENCOUNTER

The major disadvantage of telephone interviewing is the lack of nonverbal communication — smiles, puzzled looks, raised eyebrows — which, according to some research, forms 60% of total interpersonal communication messages. As a result, there may be more embarrassing silences, unintentional interruptions, or misinterpretations of tone. Candidates may also be less well prepared mentally because of the lack of formality and ritual associated with a face-to-face interview, held outside their own home. And these disadvantages can apply to both sides — the company may not be presented in its best light either.

WHERE IS THE EVIDENCE?

Dr Joanne Silvester of the Department of Psychology at City University, London, is an experienced researcher in recruitment practices. She and a team of researchers from the University of Wales and Goldsmiths College compared decision-making and the reliability of telephone and face-to-face selection interviews during the graduate recruitment "milk round", by the UK operation of multinational oil corporation Shell[2].

The team wanted to know whether people interviewed over the phone were either advantaged or disadvantaged by its use. While the focus was on graduate recruitment, the results have implications across the entire recruitment spectrum.

Silvester comments: "Research carried out in the 1970s showed that people who conduct interviews or communicate over the phone in general are more task-focused — concentrating on content rather than interpersonal aspects. In discussions over the telephone, the stronger arguments win through. Where you are in a one-to-one situation, you can influence things much more effectively. The outcome is not so dependent on the strength of your argument" — a point in favour of telephone interviewing.

And while both candidates and interviewers report that they like to know who they are talking to, Silvester notes that: "The other side of that is that interviewers can be influenced by appearances. So it could be a good thing to do telephone interviews on the basis of that."

Study findings

The main finding of her research was that candidates interviewed by phone are consistently rated worse after a face-to-face interview, regardless of any other factors.

However, Silvester points out that the researchers do not know which of those ratings was the most valid: "It could be that if you follow the arguments that telephone interviews focus more on the facts than the interpersonal, then the interview is actually, in one sense, more valid."

She also points out that, in practice, the difference does not matter, providing all candidates receive their interview by the same method – either telephone or face to face.

In general, interviewers reported enjoying the experience of telephone interviewing, and felt it was useful in improving their own performance as interviewers. The candidates themselves were not as enthusiastic, finding the lack of feedback offputting and seeing telephone interviewing as more appropriate as a screening process prior to a face-to-face interview.

Practical implications

The message for employers is to be consistent. And in the case of telephone interviewing, it is necessary to train interviewers, some of whom can be uncomfortable with an unfamiliar process.

For the employer, telephone interviewing is quicker and cheaper, although there are hidden administrative costs associated with setting up interviews. In the study, interviewers were required to make an initial call to candidates to arrange a mutually convenient time for the telephone interview. "But in many cases, candidates were not easily contactable and several phone calls were required before interviewers were finally able to arrange an interview time."

Difficulties can also arise when candidates do not have access to a private phone – often the case for students, for example – and cannot arrange a suitable location for a telephone interview.

Silvester sees further implications relating to the market in which the organisation is operating: "The question is whether they are in a sell or buy mode. If they're operating in a market where demand exceeds supply, they will need to go into selling mode to attract good people. In this situation, a telephone interview may not impress a candidate, because it's less personal and much more difficult for them to get an idea of what the organisation is about." And where the process is outsourced, that problem is magnified. "It's important to bear in mind that this is a two-way process – a chance for the candidate to understand what the culture of the organisation is. Where there is a pool of applicants, it's not such a problem. But you need to understand your market."

CASE STUDY

Centrica: the case for equity

One company that has used telephone interviewing to gain access to previously untapped sources of skills is energy supply and home services company Centrica. The company used telephone interviewing as the initial selection technique in a project launched under the New Deal scheme and backed by the Carers' National Association, the Employers' Forum on Disability, the Employment Service and outplacement and training specialist Capita Grosvenor. The aim was to ensure objectivity and remove the need for applicants to travel. Candidates with hearing disabilities were interviewed by minicom.

The New Deal is a government initiative to give young people, long-term unemployed adults and people with disabilities greater opportunities to get into work. At Centrica, there was a sound business rationale for getting involved in the project. The company needs a large number of people to operate its two call centres in Manchester and its bill-processing departments in Oldham and Hattersley, and often experiences difficulty in finding people with the right skills and qualities.

Interviewed by *People Management* magazine[3], Centrica's HR manager Jill Sheldon said that the company's usual recruitment process was failing to encourage large numbers of applications from groups "who are generally ignored by employers. We were missing potentially high-performing employees, and that was a loss to us as well as to them."

The scheme involved encouraging unemployed people with disabilities to apply for New Deal traineeships. The potential pool of talent included their carers. All applicants took part in a structured telephone interview, lasting about 20 minutes, to identify their suitability for one of the posts on offer. From around 300 applicants, about 100 were selected to proceed to the next stage of the process: a two-day "work-preparation module". The project resulted in the successful employment of 47 people in Centrica's Manchester operations.

A key part of the process relating to the initial telephone interview was that those who were unsuccessful were given feedback to help them in future applications with other employers.

CASE STUDY

EDS: the case for efficiency

EDS is an IT services provider that offers offshoot services via an outsourcing function – from managing call centres to running IT departments and providing consultancy services. Customers include the Inland Revenue, BP, the Department for Work and Pensions and Rolls-Royce. The company reported revenues of $21.5 billion in 2001. It employs around 140,000 people worldwide, 21,000 of whom are based in the UK.

LCM Recruitment (Leadership Change Management) is the HR function of EDS. Recruitment is decentralised and operates through regional recruitment teams. To ensure consistency of standards and procedures, LCM sets the strategies and systems and determines the processes to be used.

Telephone recruitment practices

Telephone screening is a key preselection tool for EDS. According to the company, the advantages of using telephone screening are that it:

- enables shortlisting of candidates in a way that is efficient and effective for both the applicants and the company;

- offers particular value when preselecting for vacancies where telephone manner and customer contact are key competencies, such as roles in call and contact centres;

- provides a more accurate assessment of the applicant's match with job-related criteria (for example, checking multilingual skills); and

- provides an interactive medium, as opposed to form-based screening.

EDS identifies few disadvantages when telephone interviewing is used solely for pre-screening. The loss of nonverbal communication is seen as the principal drawback.

The company believes that, as with any interview technique, the format must be well structured to achieve the best results. EDS sees telephone interviewing as being a cost-effective and flexible recruitment tool, and one that has become an essential part of its hiring process. However, it feels it should be used only as a pre-screening method, and not as a main selection tool: "You will never get the full picture from a telephone screening."

CASE STUDY

Scottish Equitable: the case for economy

Financial services company Scottish Equitable was bought in the early 1990s by larger Dutch insurance company Aegon, which also owns several other UK companies. Scottish Equitable represents around 50% of Aegon's UK business, and handles all its recruitment. Offices are located in Scotland, England and Northern Ireland, employing some 3,000 people in all.

Diverse recruitment activities range across all business functions, from mail loggers to customer servicing, IT, legal, sales and senior management. The company has a very positive attitude to telephone screening as a cost-effective recruitment tool.

Telephone recruitment practices

Entry-level telephone screening is currently outsourced through an agency in Edinburgh, and comprises a basic check of work history, mobility and career aspirations, including some competency-based questions.

All other professional-level positions are screened by in-house staff, with interviews lasting up to an hour. There is a some attention to work experience, but the main focus is on critical competencies and requirements for the job, both technical and behavioural. Data collected are restricted to "need-to-know" details – name, address, salary and where the candidate would be willing to work. Psychometric testing is done at a later stage, and not via the telephone.

According to HR manager Greg Fletcher, his company is "able to get a much better match with the candidate" prior to a face-to-face interview. To ensure the process is both consistent and equitable, "it doesn't matter if the person works across the street. The first step in the process is going to be a telephone screening."

The pros

According to Scottish Equitable, the advantages of using telephone screening are that it:

- enables a much better candidate match, reducing the need for in-house interviews;

- constitutes an equitable process;

- minimises interview stress;

- produces a saving of interview time and costs with a reduction in interview numbers;

- offers a means of recruitment at a significantly lower cost than using an employment agency;

- facilitates the vetting of candidates from non-traditional sources (that is, other than agency referral, where pre-vetting has already been done); and

- achieves a recruitment success ratio of four in 10 as opposed to one in 10 without telephone screening.

Not all areas of Scottish Equitable's business use telephone screening to the same degree. For example, customer services uses it primarily at entry level, and outsources some assessment functions. However, for Aegon UK, the parent company, phone screening is a prerequisite of all recruitment.

The cons

According to Scottish Equitable, there are no disadvantages when telephone interviewing is used as a pre-screening tool. It does not use phone screening at the secondary level of recruitment. While the company agrees that lack of familiarity with phone screening can mean some people – both applicants and interviewers – are initially uncomfortable with the process, the response is very positive once the benefits become clear.

Sources

1. Recruitment and retention 2002, survey report, May 2002, Chartered Institute of Personnel and Development.

2. A cross-modal comparison of telephone and face-to-face selection interviews in graduate recruitment, Joanne Silvester et al, Blackwell Publishers Ltd, March 2000.

3. "Energy efficient", Mark Whitehead, *People Management*, 11 November 1999, available at www.peoplemanagement.co.uk.

Chapter 10
Online selection

Though online recruitment remains a lasting legacy of the dotcom bubble, with one survey by the Chartered Institute of Personnel and Development[1] suggesting 75% of employers make some use of email or the web to attract applicants, online selection remains far more rare. The survey, which covered nearly 1,000 organisations, found just 1% tested applicants online while 1.9% offered web-based self-testing facilities to applicants.

This chapter looks at some of the issues facing these pioneering companies and the sometimes unexpected challenges that have been thrown up in the process. It then goes on to look at the experience of two major employers: consultants KPMG and high street bank Abbey National.

THE CASE FOR ONLINE SELECTION

- Online testing and self-testing allows applicants to be easily matched against pre-set criteria and unsuitable applicants to be weeded out at an early stage.

- By going back to basics and rethinking their recruitment processes, employers are able to strip out questions that have little relevance to the final decision.

- It opens up vacancies to a wider, international audience who might otherwise be missed.

THE CASE AGAINST ONLINE SELECTION

- Shifting selection online requires a complete rethink of the employer's approach – it's not just a matter of moving paper systems onto a computer.

- With so few employers adopting this approach, there is little experience to learn from.

- Concerns remain about the ability of the technology now available to perform reliably and to expectations.

EARLY LESSONS FROM THE PIONEERS

Online selection has the potential to be more accurate, faster and more cost effective than traditional approaches. It allows employers to develop better profiles both of the jobs they are trying to fill and the candidates who are applying for them. And it can help to verify test validity, minimise discriminatory questioning and strengthen predictability.

To date, the first companies to move to online selection have found most of their problems involve finding suitable technology to support and manage their systems. But they have also faced the need to revamp their recruitment processes and manage the impact of the changes on the roles of staff involved in recruitment.

They also point out that the benefits must be balanced against the expense and difficulty of creating an information technology infrastructure that maintains the security of the site and prevents unauthorised access to test data. Also, the system must allow the retrieval of personal information about individual candidates, to which, under data protection legislation, they have rights of access.

Essentially, using online recruitment and selection is an end result, not a starting point. Creating an infrastructure to support the system, the staff and the candidates using it is vital. The recruitment process itself will also need reworking – it has become clear that moving a paper-based application form online is not satisfactory, either for those administering it or those completing it.

SECURITY AND RISK MANAGEMENT

Dr Robert Sternberg, director of the Yale Centre for the Psychology of Abilities, Competencies and Expertise, and professor of psychology and education at Yale University, believes that psychometric testing can be facilitated satisfactorily online "as long as appropriate security arrangements are made".

He urges employers to take steps to ensure:

- that the person taking the test is the person who is supposed to be taking the test;
- that the conditions of testing are as they are supposed to be; and
- that items are not being copied and their security is upheld.

Many organisations retest a random sample of applicants who get through the screening process in a bid to stamp out cheating. Wild differences in the same candidate's scores for the two tests will result in either revoking a job offer or disqualifying the candidate from the recruitment process. The candidate will be made aware of this through an honesty contract that appears in the introduction to the test.

Other security measures that can be used include the use of passwords to protect test sites and, probably the most effective, the development of software that ensures each test is unique, and recreated every time someone takes the test, so that candidates cannot simply download questions and work out answers in advance before submitting their application.

RETHINKING THE APPLICATION

Many companies try to translate their paper-based application process onto the internet either in its original form or by following a hybrid approach that results in considerable duplication and paperwork. Such systems tend not to work, proving convoluted, time-consuming, clumsy for candidates and frustrating for the employer.

After reviewing its approach and removing much of the extraneous information included in its paper-based application forms, KPMG found that it could reduce the time taken to complete an application online from three hours to just one.

The rethink also prompted the company to develop a standard profile that acts as a benchmark. By answering a series of 128 questions, the candidate gives enough information to generate a profile, which is scored against the benchmark profile. The system then makes an automatic recommendation either to move the candidate to the next stage of the process or reject them. As a back-up, however, the HR department still goes through each application individually.

POINTS TO REMEMBER

Those who adopted online selection early on can look back and reflect on the things they now wish they had known at the start. Among the key pieces of advice they offer are:

- Remember that online selection is a tool to aid judgment – they do not provide a judgment in itself.
- Give yourself time to plan and test your new system.
- Don't believe suppliers who insist they can have a programme up and running within eight weeks – they can but you'll be ironing out problems on the move.
- Take the opportunity of moving online to re-engineer your recruitment process.

CASE STUDY

KPMG's graduate recruitment programme

KPMG is a global network of professional services firms operating from 24 offices across the UK. It has more than 12,000 partners and staff and had fee income of £1.4 billion in the UK in year ended September 2001.

"I think our decision to go online for graduate recruitment and screening was very much in the context of the e-business revolution," explains Keith Dugdale Dugdale, director, national graduate recruitment at KPMG. The company was becoming heavily involved in developing e-business solutions with, and for, clients and it felt it needed to "walk the talk" with regard to using technology within its own business.

"The second reason was that we were very conscious of the fact that we needed to be much quicker and much smarter in the way that we recruited. We were dealing with huge volumes of applications – 7,000 or 8,000 per year for 650 jobs – so we needed systems that could cope effectively."

Keith Dugdale continues: "The third reason we went down this route is that we had a model which invested huge amounts of time, money and resources in actually rejecting people in the most sophisticated way possible. The model was a model built on rejection, not a model built on selection."

KPMG took the opportunity to study the process it uses and make changes to ensure it "had a model where we invested our time, energy and money in recruiting those people we wanted to recruit. And, on the other hand, in the most sophisticated and consistent way possible, reject those people we wanted to reject quickly. Recruitment now is about developing positive relationships with candidates, both potential and real," says Keith Dugdale.

Another important aspect of the recruitment process that KPMG wanted to improve related to providing feedback to all applicants – both successful and unsuccessful.

Getting started

Once the company had established that it wanted to go down the route of online recruitment and screening, it found it difficult to find suppliers who could provide a system that met the needs of both mainstream recruitment and graduate recruitment. The company made a decision that, at that time, the priority was to get the recruitment and selection of graduates online.

In order to go online by September 2000, the company began looking at various suppliers in the marketplace, while also working internally with the graduate recruitment team. Keith Dugdale reckons this was a very important part of the process – getting the graduate recruitment team on board – and, initially, members of the team had a "whole host of concerns - would students apply online? Would the IT stand up to it?" But there were also concerns about the way the changes would affect them and their job roles."

Once the company had decided on a supplier – an organisation it had worked with in the past and felt confident with – KPMG began looking at the old process and stripping it down to ensure the essentials were included, and not much else. The company had learned from its mistake a year earlier when it had gone online and had "just taken our existing paper-based application form and put it online. Keith Dugdale says: "We really gutted the application form and got it back to its core. We had been seeking a whole plethora of information which we weren't using to make decisions – or, if we were, we shouldn't have been because it was subjective."

Self-profiling: the first stage

An integral part of the application process is a self-reporting profiling tool where applicants are asked to rate themselves – using a scoring system – in a series of 128 questions.

The graduate recruitment team had spent time working with an occupational psychology firm developing a profile of what it was looking for in terms of competencies. This profile is used as a benchmark against which students and applicants are then scored. "This was a very radical departure, and I think that was at the heart of our new approach. It is totally objective – you either match the profile or not," says Keith Dugdale.

He goes on: "This self-profile is integral to the application process, so everyone completes it. That's the way we were able to generate feedback based on that profile, because you could say, in comparison to 7,000 other people who applied to KPMG, your profile is strong here and weak here."

The graduate recruitment team had assumed that moving entirely online would reduce the number of applications quite substantially. However, this has not been the case, as Keith Dugdale points out: "Instead, the profile of our applicants has changed and we now get a lot more international applicants than we previously had because of the access to the web." In fact, the number of graduate applicants that KPMG attracts increased.

Human back-up

Once candidates have completed the online application, including the self-assessment profile, the system "scores" the applicant against the benchmark profile and offers a recommendation as to whether to reject the candidate at this stage or take them through to the next phase.

The graduate recruitment team looks at each candidate's application and undertakes a second review. Keith Dugdale explains: "We feel that this is important and was particularly important during the first year, because people had to have confidence in the system and had to see it operating. There are so many nuances to recruitment that actually human intervention at that point in time is the sensible and rational thing to do."

The evolving process

"We've been learning all the time. Last year, for example, our application form was buried on the website. We made the fundamental mistake of thinking applicants should find out all about the company and get all the information first and then apply, but feedback led us to believe that it takes too long to get to the application form. Now we've set it up so that you can click straight to the application form and bypass everything else."

Keith Dugdale and his team have also put in place a feedback loop to ensure that they are always hearing from those who are using the application process. There are focus groups conducted with: the entire population of those who applied; those who were offered jobs but rejected KPMG; and those who were successful.

Cost benefits

There have been some significant cost savings: the headcount of those involved in graduate recruitment has been reduced by about 20%, and fewer people are being called to first interview and the assessment centre – "that's a big cost for us because it involves a lot of live time," says Keith Dugdale.

CASE STUDY

Abbey National

Abbey National has operated a fully interactive online application process since October 2001. This is competency-based, and includes a screening tool for the recruitment of branch-based financial advisers and call centre advisers. The online process has replaced the shortlisting process, and has been completely reworked.

According to Maureen Hinks, recruitment manager at Abbey National, "the main problems have been around managing the database [which supports the screening system] and the candidates' perception of the process, that is, using the internet rather than having personal contact."

However, such technology problems are unlikely to feature as strongly in future as systems develop and more models of practice become available.

Abbey National did have to make one unforeseen change in its approach to recruitment. Maureen Hinks says: "The role of the recruitment consultant changed significantly, in that we were asking consultants to change from reactive recruiting to proactively sourcing. And we've had to introduce a new role to manage the database.

"Initially, we asked a number of the consultants to 'manage' the candidate database, which required them to spend more time at their computers. This involved making decisions about whether to take applicants forward to the next stage. We were also asking them to develop relationships with candidates prior to there being a vacancy. This was a very different approach to normal."

Within Abbey National, the application process was also reworked, with the application form rationalised and based on competencies. The screening tool presents the candidate with a variety of scenarios and asks them to choose the response they would be most likely to give. This information allows recruitment consultants to predict typical performance.

It is still early days to assess the full impact of the move online, but Maureen Hinks comments: "The early signs are good. The call centre adviser process has generated more hires at this stage. And, generally, feedback has been positive; we now have the potential to recruit people faster – as long as the candidate database is managed effectively."

She goes on: "I think candidates also receive a better 'feel' for the role by going through the role-related scenarios. I think most candidates would probably say it was 'slicker' and gave them more information about the role and the company culture."

Sources

1. Recruitment and retention 2002, survey report, May 2002, Chartered Institute of Personnel and Development.

Chapter 11
Psychometric testing

All recruitment decisions carry a risk. The more business-critical the vacancy, the more expensive a mistake can be, so the theory goes. Employing more than one selection method has been shown to minimise – although not eliminate – the risks. Although the interview continues to be the most often used selection method, it remains a poor predictor of likely success in a role. In the right context, occupational testing – otherwise known as psychometric testing – can lead to better employment decisions based on objective results, and not subjective opinions.

This chapter looks at the debate about the pros and cons of psychometric testing and reports the findings of an IRS study of employer practices. It also offers an introduction to the legal issues involved.

THE CASE FOR PSYCHOMETRIC TESTING

- Its use is widespread and as one of a range of selection methods offers the opportunity of recruiting more appropriate candidates to fill vacancies.

- New and better designed psychometric tests can reduce the risk of bias and unlawful discrimination.

THE CASE AGAINST PSYCHOMETRIC TESTING

- Devising any system of psychometric tests requires professional expertise likely to be available only outside the organisation.

- Great care must be taken to follow guidance issued by the British Psychological Society and to meet all legal requirements for equal opportunities and data protection.

- Online testing presents problems verifying candidates' identity, raises security concerns about unauthorised access to test data, and means candidates must be given access to personal information stored about them.

WHO USES PSYCHOMETRIC TESTS?

According to the Institute of Directors, psychometric tests are used by more than 700 of the *The Times*' top 1,000 companies[1]. Indeed, the Chartered Institute of Personnel and Development (CIPD)[2] reports that 60% of job applicants for management roles will face psychometric testing. The main types of tests include:

- personality (aims to measure social skills, teamworking, motivation, adaptation and resilience, by looking at extraversion, emotional stability, agreeableness, conscientiousness and culture);

- IQ (aims to measure intelligence);

- aptitude (aims to measure specific skills such as numerical or verbal reasoning); and

- emotional intelligence (aims to measure self-awareness, emotional control, self-motivation, empathy with others, and the ability to understand and inspire others).

IRS research[3] involving 61 employers about the tools they use to select new employees shows that psychometric testing appears to be a firmly embedded part of the selection process. Four out of five employers use testing when selecting candidates. More than half of this group have increased their level of testing over the past two years.

WHAT ARE EMPLOYERS DOING?

IRS found that selection testing appears to be firmly embedded within organisations as a part of the selection process. Four out of five employers use testing when selecting candidates. More than half of those had increased the level of testing undertaken within their organisation over the past two years.

Ability/aptitude tests

Seven in 10 employers use ability or aptitude tests to aid the selection process. These tests rank third in terms of usage after interviews and application forms and are ahead of CVs. Employers remain selective about using ability and aptitude tests, with only 8% using the tests for all job roles. It is when recruiting managers or people into managerial positions that this kind of testing is most used, with almost half of all employers using such tests for these positions.

Literacy and numeracy tests

Basic tests designed to assess candidates' literacy and numeracy are used by more than half of employers and one in 10 use such testing for every job role.

Even though there is an increasing trend towards testing, employers are still reluctant to base their decisions on the results of these tests alone. Just 2% of employers felt it is the selection method that has the most influence on their decisions. However, only 4% of employers felt that literacy and numeracy tests have the least influence on their decision-making process, perhaps a better indication of how employers feel about these tests.

Personality questionnaires

Personality tests add another dimension to the selection process by providing extra insight into a person's character. However, a qualified test administrator – capable of understanding what is being measured, and interpreting and applying the results, along with the ethics and legalities – should use or advise on this method.

This mainly qualitative selection method is used by almost two-thirds of employers. It is when choosing managers that personality questionnaires are most often used - one in four employers indicated they employ personality questionnaires when selecting for these positions.

In line with recommended good practice, employers do not appear to be using personality testing in isolation. In fact, many employers indicated that they felt such tests have the least influence on their selection decisions.

Thinking it through

Reasons given by employers for using selection testing include using it as an extra tool to add a further dimension to the selection process and to help avoid making costly mistakes. One employer told IRS: "Recruitment where testing has been used is now showing good fit and retention." Another said that using such testing "improves that quality of recruits by gaining a more objective and more well-rounded viewpoint".

Employers are not keen to provide job applicants with samples of the tests that will be used in the selection process. Even though it is considered best practice to ensure candidates are warned of the testing methods being used, just under half of employers send samples to them in advance.

Offering feedback is also thought of as best practice. It allows the candidate the opportunity to explore the results of tests with qualified personnel. Employers appear to be conscientious about this aspect of testing, just under half of those using testing always offer feedback to candidates. More than four in 10 do so when it has been requested by the candidate and only one employer in our survey never offers feedback.

ONLINE TESTING

The emergence of the internet as an everyday business tool has opened the way for more widespread use of psychometric testing. Chapter 10 looked at how some employers have already taken that opportunity. However few employers studied by IRS have done so, and almost half of all respondents objected to selection tests being administered online, for a variety of reasons. Many spoke of the poor practices that they perceive the use of online testing can cause; others felt that it is a cold and "hands-off" approach to testing.

One public sector organisation, with 3,500 staff, told us that: "Online testing is open to misuse as candidates could have received help in completing the test." Another public sector organisation felt that online selection is "impossible to administer over the internet". Others spoke of the inability to control the process and the environment in which the tester is taking part.

But these findings are in contrast to research conducted by test-provider and developer ASE. Its survey of 160 UK organisations – covering most major industries but mainly involving those employing more than 500 individuals – showed that almost two in three psychometric test users were interested in making use of the electronic versions of tests.

According to ASE's managing director, Ian Florance: "The internet breaks down national barriers and suggests new ways of organising, communicating and linking information." He also feels that it democratises testing. But also that it "makes available powerful and potentially damaging instruments which people cannot cope with" without any quality or validity requirement.

The advantages of this type of testing include immediate feedback and lower delivery costs, which can make testing jobs more affordable for lower-paid jobs. Even on the question of validity, storing data centrally among application service providers can actually help to verify test validity, minimise discriminatory questioning and strengthen predictability.

THE FUTURE

Security and the internet

Test developers are working to increase the use of the internet in occupational testing – in a variety of ways. Oxford Psychologists Press is developing a system that will allow managers to assess candidates using a combination of computer-based tests and telephone testing, administered with software sent via email. ASE is developing a programme in conjunction with totaljobs.com, one of the major commercial recruitment websites, to improve the selection process on its jobs board.

ASE is also working to improve security on the internet and ensure that interfering either in the test process or the results becomes a thing of the past. SHL, another major test publisher, has produced a numeracy test that issues random questions that make it a unique test for each applicant.

Of course, foul play in occupational testing is not necessarily a new thing. Individuals have had the opportunity to go on "training courses" to perform "well" in psychometric tests for some time now. The test developers have also responded to this, and have increased the sophistication of the tests and included such things as impression management – which allows the test interpreter to pick up unusual patterns in responses.

New testing techniques

Cognitive Processes Profile, developed in South Africa by Maretha Prinsloo of Magellan Consulting, is a computerised simulation exercise that provides an insight into: cognitive style (whether the approach adopted to thinking is intuitive or analytical); what areas of thinking can be developed to tackle tasks; and the individual's ideal (current and potential) work environment.

Ian Florance of ASE explains: "Traditionally, tests have given a slice through people at a specific time: their personality and abilities as they took the test. But as we understand more about processes in the brain and find how genes affect our development, we can begin to measure process and, therefore, genuinely look at how people can and cannot be developed.

"Measurement of process is, I think, going to become the test subject of the future, not least because in fast-changing organisations, static ability at a certain time cannot predict achievement six months down the line in a completely different organisation."

CPP has been designed to overcome the bias involved in conventional IQ testing. Whereas, with IQ tests, individuals are presented with structured content that requires an analytical style or approach in order to come to an answer, CPP has been developed to present information in a different way. The information can be vague and a series of clues are included, some of which are ambiguous and can be interpreted using any stylistic approach. Fundamentally, no "correct" answer is required from the individual taking the test. It is not necessarily the answer chosen that is the indicator but, rather, the thought process that was involved in choosing or arriving at the answer.

The 16 cognitive styles covered by CPP are: analytical; balanced; efficient; explorative; general; holistic; impulsive; integrative; intuitive; learning; logical; memory; metaphoric; random; reflective; and structured.

A NOTE ON THE LAW

Psychometric testing now comes under more legislation than ever before – regardless of the medium used to deliver or administer the tests. Primarily, organisations need to ensure that they do not fall foul of anti-discrimination laws or the implications of the data protection legislation, particularly when using automated selection systems and in the processing of test data[4].

It is also important for good practice that tests are administered by qualified test users. The Steering Committee on Test Standards - part of the British Psychological Society – has produced two sets of standards for the use of tests in the occupational setting[5]. The Level A standards cover basic psychometric principles and the skills required to use attainment and ability tests, and the Level B Standards cover more advanced psychometric principles and the skills required to use tests of personality and interest. It is expected that it will become a legal requirement to use qualified test users in the future.

The testing process is complex and requires a high level of commitment on the part of the organisation. But correct training is vital to try to protect the organisation.

Sex and race discrimination

The Sex Discrimination Act 1975 and the Race Relations Act 1976 prohibit discrimination at every stage of employment, including the recruitment and selection process. The Equal Opportunities Commission's: *Code of Practice on sex discrimination: equal opportunity policies, procedures and practices in employment* (1985) recommends the establishment and use of consistent criteria for selection and promotion. These criteria can remove much of the subjectivity around selection decisions that can lead to unlawful discrimination. Indirect sex discrimination can occur in selection testing because of differences between men and women in their response to psychometric questionnaires.

The Code is clear that selection tests should be specifically related to job and/or career requirements, and should measure an individual's actual or inherent ability to do or train for the work or career. It recommends that tests should be reviewed regularly to ensure that they remain relevant and free from any unjustifiable bias, either in content or scoring mechanism.

The Commission for Racial Equality, in its *Code of Practice for the elimination of racial discrimination and the promotion of equality of opportunity in employment* (1983), recommends:

- the adoption, implementation and monitoring of an equal opportunities policy to ensure that no job applicant receives less favourable treatment on racial grounds or is placed at a disadvantage by requirements or conditions with a disproportionately adverse effect on his or her racial group;

- the examination of selection criteria and tests to ensure that they are related to job requirements and are not unlawfully discriminatory. For example, "selection tests which contain irrelevant questions or exercises on matters which may be unfamiliar to racial minority applicants should not be used (for example, general knowledge questions on matters more likely to be familiar to indigenous applicants)"; and

- staff responsible for shortlisting, interviewing and selecting candidates should be: clearly informed of selection criteria and of the need for their consistent application; given guidance or training on the effects that generalised assumptions and prejudices about race can have on selection decisions; and made aware of the possible misunderstandings that can occur in interviews between persons of different cultural backgrounds.

Codes of Practice are admissible in evidence in tribunal and court proceedings, and any provision relevant to questions arising in the proceedings may be taken into account by the tribunal or court in determining those questions.

Testing disabled employees

Employers using occupational testing need to ensure that they do not unfairly or unjustifiably screen out disabled job applicants. Blind people or those with severe visual impairment may be screened out by tests requiring abstract reasoning. Deaf people or those with a severe hearing impairment who communicate by means of sign language rather than spoken English may be screened out by verbal reasoning, spelling and/or grammar tests. Personality questionnaires may screen out applicants who have a mental illness or a history of mental illness and who may score negatively on a measure of "emotional stability".

The duty of "reasonable adjustment" referred to in the Disability Discrimination Act 1995 puts the onus on the employer to ensure that disabled people are accommodated in arrangements for recruitment and selection. Employers are also required to avoid "less favourable treatment" of disabled candidates and must seek to comply with the duty of "reasonable adjustment".

Data protection

The Data Protection Act 1998 applies to occupational or psychometric testing that involves the processing of personal data – information from which a living person can be identified (or can be identified from that data in conjunction with other information in the possession, or likely to come into the possession, of the data controller).

Employers must comply with the data protection principles in relation to all personal data in their control. This means that all personal data must:

- be processed fairly and lawfully;

- be obtained only for one or more specified and lawful purposes, and must not be processed in any manner incompatible with that or those purposes;

- be adequate, relevant and not excessive in relation to the purpose(s) for which the data are processed;

- be accurate and, where necessary, kept up to date;

- not be kept any longer than is necessary for that purpose or those purposes;

- be processed in accordance with the employee's rights under the Act;

- be protected against unauthorised or unlawful processing, and against accidental loss, destruction or damage; and,

- not be transferred outside the EU without an adequate level of protection for employees.

Sources

1. People Management online, Research Centre, 23 October 2001, www.peoplemanagement.co.uk/archiveitem.asp?id=1408.

2. People Management online, Research Centre, 23 October 2001, www.peoplemanagement.co.uk/archiveitem.asp?id=1408.

3. "Psychometrics: the next generation", *IRS Employment Review* 744, January 2002.

4. Further information on the Data Protection Act Code of Practice can be found on the internet at www.dataprotection.gov.uk.

5. The British Psychological Society can be contacted at St Andrews House, 48 Princess Road East, Leicester LE1 7DR, tel: 0116 254 9568, website: www.bps.org.uk.

Chapter 12
Assessment centres

Assessment centres bring together a powerful mix of different selection methods, and assess groups of candidates over an extended period of up to two days at a time. Since their creation by the military in the Second World War, they have been adopted by many employers and an estimated one in three now uses them. But their power depends on careful and skilled preparation, and an investment of considerable amounts of time, effort and money. Assessment centres have gained a reputation as the Rolls-Royce of selection methods. Like the luxury cars, they are expensive to design, run and maintain, but can be highly efficient in what they do.

In this chapter, we look at ways to make the most of assessment centres and provide three real-life examples, drawn from the varied backgrounds of a manufacturer, a high-street retailer and a government department.

THE CASE FOR ASSESSMENT CENTRES

- They are more likely than other methods to identify the right candidate for the job.

- More than half of all organisations that recruit graduates use assessment centres, making them an industry standard.

THE CASE AGAINST ASSESSMENT CENTRES

- They are expensive, time consuming and difficult to organise.

- A poorly designed centre can reflect badly on your organisation.

WHAT IS AN ASSESSMENT CENTRE

There is no single definition of an "assessment centre", but there is general agreement that it involves all of the following elements:

- a group of candidates are brought together at the same time and place;

- the same series of selection processes is undergone by each candidate;

- these methods involve a combination of collective and individual selection techniques;

- the selection methods are designed to reveal how candidates would perform in the organisation;

- the selection methods are designed around the actual demands of the vacancy;

- the performance of the candidates is evaluated by at least two assessors; and

- the event is sustained over a relatively long period.

The key point, though, is that assessment centres are a fair selection method. Candidates are assessed in more than one situation, against pre-determined, objective criteria, and by more than one assessor.

Designing and running an assessment centre requires considerable investment in time, resources and – in all but the largest organisations with their in-house experts – the input of a suitably experienced and qualified external adviser. The assessors, all or most of whom are usually managers from the host organisation, have to be trained and then must find the time to run the centre. The organisation is asking a great deal of the candidates themselves, as well as of its own managers, and should be prepared to offer successful and unsuccessful candidates alike in-depth feedback on their performance. If assessors know that their judgments will be passed on to the candidate, this can help maintain the discipline of ensuring that assessments are as objective as possible.

Attempts to short-circuit any of these steps not only undermine the effectiveness of the centre – in effect, the investment will be wasted because poor appointment decisions will be the result – but can also inflict psychological damage on the participants. An assessment centre is an intense experience for candidates, requiring a great deal of commitment and energy. If it is mishandled, the reputation of the organisation will be undermined.

MAKING THE MOST OF ASSESSMENT CENTRES

Guidelines

At present, there are no best-practice recommendations or code of conduct governing the general use of assessment centres in the UK. In 1989, the US Task Force on Assessment Center Guidelines produced a series of standards for that country. In the UK, the British Psychological Society's working party is still formulating its proposals, although the Association of Graduate Recruiters has published a briefing on the use of centres in graduate recruitment[1]. However, most British researchers writing on the subject have set out what they see as the key issues and a synthesis of these points is shown in our checklist below.

Making assessment centres relevant

Many employers are now adapting their assessment centres to build in greater work relevance; they know that close linkages between the centre's design and the requirements of the job help to improve its ability to identify the most suitable applicants.

A study of assessment centres for the Cabinet Office[2], as part of a recent project to improve the Civil Service Fast Stream, found that "it seemed to be important to all recruiters that candidates visited their offices at some point to get a feel for the organisation and its people, its atmosphere and culture". As a result, assessment centres tended to take place in a convenient location nearby. At Pret a Manger, the fast-food retailer and one of our case studies, each external assessment centre begins at 6.30am in one of the company's shops, where candidates "shadow" a manager or team leader for four hours.

Similarly, many employers try to ensure that the exercises and interviews in their centres more closely reflect real life in the organisation. They are checking that the centres capture the reality of the skills required. And simulations are being used more extensively and realistically. At the Halifax, a major financial services company, the company's external advisers helped it modify its assessment centre into a single simulation: a seven-hour business scenario[3].

Sharpening assessment centre design

Centres that consist of a series of self-contained exercises lose some of their ability to provide a realistic insight into the job and candidates' potential performance in it, and can be disruptive for participants. Consequently, efforts are being made to ensure that each exercise flows into the next, and, where simulations or scenarios are used, that each exercise uses the same context – the same business challenge, or fictitious people and events.

Rapid organisational change, and the likelihood that it will continue in the future, has focused some organisations' attention on core values. Given that jobs, roles and the tasks involved are likely to change significantly, it becomes more important to consider the core values underlying the organisation's activities, and to take account of them in the assessment centre. Both employer and candidate stand to gain if their values are shown to coincide.

Some employers now administer some or all of the psychometric tests they used to include in their centres at a previous stage of the selection process. This makes the best use of the time available in the centre, and still allows the test results to form part of the information used in making assessments.

Focusing on candidates

Assessment centres that are seen to make unreasonable demands of candidates mean that applicants may go elsewhere, and many users of assessment centres have been trying to reduce the length of their recruitment process, so that sought-after applicants do not lose interest and take up a job offer from a competitor.

Selection of applicants to be called to a centre also provides opportunities to improve both the centre's effectiveness and the candidate-friendly nature of the recruitment system. Centres are expensive to run, and it is rarely possible or desirable to invite all applicants to attend. As a result, some employers have improved their selection techniques to ensure that this sifting is as objective and effective as possible. Some employers have enhanced their application forms, for example, by including more questions directly linked to the dimensions used in their assessment centres.

Applicant selection takes on an added dimension where a centre involves both external and internal applicants. The two groups may not be compatible. Internal candidates have an inside knowledge of the organisation, often of the job involved. They may know how to perform so as to make a favourable impression on the assessors, many of whom will be managers drawn from within the organisation, and could well already be known to the candidates.

Conversely, the organisation will know much more about internal applicants than external ones, and this may not be to their advantage. There is no guarantee that these advantages and disadvantages will cancel themselves out, and create a level playing field across the group of candidates as a whole. This has led some employers to make special provision for internal candidates.

CHECKLIST

Constructing an effective centre

- Clearly define the purpose of the assessment centre – think about internal applicants, how different aims will be reconciled and whether senior managers are on board.

- Decide whether you have sufficient expertise in-house or need to bring in external advisors to design and conduct your assessment centre.

- Determine the basis of assessment and precisely what you are looking for in an applicant.

- Decide whether to adopt a competency approach or one based more directly on the job in question.

- Ensure the assessment centre closely reflects your organisation's culture and reflects the demands of the job.

- Ensure that the different exercises and interviews are integrated, logically ordered and consistent for all candidates.

- Find a suitable venue and establish how long the process will take.

- Select assessors with aptitude for the role and train them extensively in what is required; where participants are required for role-play exercises, make sure they are fully briefed and trained.

- Draw up full documentation for assessors to consult as they go along and to record their observations.

- Agree a scoring method and establish the role of the assessors' post-centre discussion.

- Brief candidates on the essential details of the assessment centre.

- Decide on the content, format and style of feedback to candidates.

- Pilot the centre with volunteers.

- After the event, evaluate the way the centre worked and its outcomes.

CASE STUDY

Britvic's graduate recruitment programme

Britvic manufactures soft drinks and employs around 2,700 staff in a number of UK locations. The company runs assessment centres predominantly for recruitment to its young manager graduate and mature graduate training programmes. Recruits to the mature programme must have at least 18 months' relevant work experience and are employed in the operations side of the business - engineering, for example. Graduates on the young manager programme are recruited to business functions, such as sales and marketing, finance and purchasing.

Britvic is a well-known brand; its recruitment programmes attract a great deal of interest, and the company aims to select the highest-calibre graduates to participate in them. Selection is a rigorous and intensive process, with more than 70 candidates being assessed for around six vacancies on its young manager graduate programme annually. The assessment centre process for both programmes involves two stages, with typically half the candidates successfully making it to the second stage.

Young manager assessment centres

Up to 24 candidates a day attend the first stage of Britvic's assessment centre for its young manager programme. This takes place in the attractive setting of an old abbey in the grounds of Britvic's Norwich site. HR takes responsibility for assessing this first assessment event, with a ratio of one assessor to two candidates. The exercises are timetabled to ensure that as many different assessors as possible observe the candidates in the course of the day.

Candidates attending all assessment centre events are closely observed against Britvic's competency framework. Each exercise is carefully selected to measure candidates against at least three of the company's six competencies. Behaviour relating to each competency is observed on three different occasions during the event.

Throughout the event, candidates tackle verbal and numerical reasoning tests. There are also one-to-one competency-based interviews and two group or "discussion" exercises. Typically, the group exercises require candidates to plan tasks and projects within a clearly defined framework and make decisions affecting specific issues or projects.

An "information event" is also included in the day. Candidates have the opportunity to meet young Britvic managers currently on the graduate programme. The assessors make a point of not being present for this part of the day. As recruitment manager Alison Cowen explains: "We feel that it is very important that would-be recruits are able to talk openly with existing employees, so that they can ask direct questions about the job and what it is like to work for Britvic."

The final "activity" exercise has a strong fun element to it. Candidates take part in a challenging practical task such as building a structure with limited materials that will support an object. All candidates, whether successful or not, are given feedback from the ability testing and on how they scored against set competencies.

The next round

The next assessment phase takes place about two weeks after the initial assessment centre. At this stage, candidates are grouped together according to the area of the business they would work in. Three different assessment days are organised with between 10 and

12 candidates attending a "sales and marketing", a "purchasing" or a "finance" assessment day.

The venue for the second stage is a management training centre. Prior to this, candidates will have completed an Occupational Personality Questionnaire. The format for the day is similar to that of the first assessment centre, with a variation in some of the exercises. For instance, on this occasion, candidates must give a 15-minute presentation. The topic for the talk, which is related to the chosen area of the business, is given to candidates in advance so that they have plenty of time to prepare.

Candidates at this selection stage are assessed by senior managers from the recruiting function, such as sales and marketing. Following a "wrap-up" session by the assessors, where they discuss their assessments of the participants, candidates are informed that evening whether they will be taken on by the company.

Mature entry

Although consisting of a similar battery of selection tests, Britvic's assessment centre for mature graduates is organised slightly differently. Fewer candidates attend one session and senior managers support the process from the outset.

"We feel that we need to invest more time in applicants who already have experience of the world of work, as this could be a serious career decision for them," explains Alison Cowen. "Therefore, the second-stage assessment centre involves an overnight stay to allow them to seek information from not only the key stakeholders of the programme but also from current programmers."

This final selection event is held at a commercial management training centre, where candidates have the opportunity to socialise in the evening with Britvic employees and may even have the chance to show off their rowing or bowling prowess.

A cost-effective option

Britvic is making a big investment in its graduate recruits. The "cost per hire" is estimated at around £2,800 per candidate. This is considered very reasonable, particularly in view of the 300% saving on previous years that this figure represents.

"The assessment centre route for selecting graduates is well worth the expenditure, and over the last year we have managed to make it even more cost-effective by streamlining the process and by the use of technology," says Alison Cowen. "We also involve a range of Britvic employees by keeping the process in-house."

CASE STUDY

Pret A Manger assesses managers on the job

Pret A Manger prides itself on selling fresh, natural food in its 120 fast-food outlets. It employs around 230 team leaders and 200 managers to run its shops, together with counter and support staff. The company aims to recruit to 60% of its management positions internally, while the remaining vacancies are filled externally.

Assessing managers

Because internal and external candidates applying for a management position may not be on an equal footing, there are two distinct assessment centre processes for each group. As Esther O'Halloran, retail recruitment manager, explains: "There is the obvious advantage to an internal candidate of being familiar with Pret's culture and modus operandi, but, conversely, our team members may not have had the opportunity to gain experience in other skills, such as giving presentations."

Pret aims to run one internal and one external assessment centre each month. The first stage of the process is the same for all candidates and consists of an application form, a psychometric test and an initial screening interview. The results of all three are taken into account before candidates undergo the assessment centre process.

The psychometric test focuses on numerical and verbal reasoning, and includes a personality questionnaire. The personality section of the questionnaire was developed with the input of around 60 Pret managers to ensure that it measures "real Pret behaviours". A software package produces a report based on the test answers that suggests specific questions to follow up with the candidate.

Back to the floor

The assessment day for external candidates kicks off at 6.30am at one of Pret's shops. The would-be manager shadows a Pret manager or team leader for four hours, learning the skills of the trade, such as making coffee and dealing with customers. In Esther O'Halloran's view, the morning session is an excellent way of getting across the reality of the job and the ethos of the organisation, which could not be achieved as effectively in an artificial setting. It also gives candidates an opportunity to assess whether the Pret environment is one they would feel comfortable working in.

Following this initiation into Pret life, the general manager responsible for the store completes a feedback sheet on the candidate's performance against set competencies.

"By the time the assessment tests start, we have a substantial set of information to inform the selection process," explains Esther O'Halloran. Candidates will have been supplied with details of what to expect at the assessment centre well in advance.

Up to eight candidates attend the centre in any one session. The ratio of assessors to candidates is high: three assessors to four or five candidates, rising to four assessors if there are six, seven or eight candidates. All assessors are Pret personnel, ranging from store managers to HR staff, who are trained to recognise the behaviours outlined in Pret's competencies.

"We like to involve Pret employees in recruitment," says Esther O'Halloran. "As well as giving them a sense of ownership of the process, they are the best people to judge whether candidates match up to our expectations."

The tests

After an initial icebreaker, the first test is a group exercise involving a "leaderless project". The group is presented with an issue or problem that needs solving by consensus, and each candidate is measured against three key competencies: leadership, communication and tenacity/resilience. Half-an-hour's preparation time is allowed.

The second exercise following a communal lunch is a one-to-one interview. Situational and behavioural questions based on Pret's competency framework follow up the results of the psychometric test and feedback form.

The final test is a presentation, made in the presence of candidates and assessors. Candidates are expected to talk on a subject that they have researched that day, using the internet. If possible, the topic is related to the food industry, and past presentations have ranged from "the history of English tea parties" to "the coffee bean". The brief is to make the presentation "interactive, visual (a flipchart is provided) and interesting". Audience participation is welcomed, as is a sense of humour.

Later, assessors have a "wash-up" where they compare notes on the suitability of candidates. A summary sheet is completed outlining people's development needs, regardless of whether they were successful. This is handed to candidates before they leave. As Pret has a rolling management recruitment programme, it will take on all the candidates attending the session who are considered suitable.

Internal candidates

Pret found that existing employees attending the assessment centre were noticeably more nervous than their external counterparts. The company has therefore developed an alternative assessment day that mirrors the assessment centre process but, instead, takes place on the job.

Candidates undertake the same exercises as external candidates, but in a work environment – such as a presentation to the shop team and an exercise that tests leadership – and are measured against the same competencies. In one sense, the management recruitment process is even more rigorous for internal candidates, as their applications must first have been endorsed by at least three Pret managers.

Team member recruitment

A scaled-down version of the assessment centre has recently been developed for candidates applying to work as team members in a new store. Around 16 candidates attend a four-hour session, where they take part in games designed to assess competencies such as teamwork, communication and listening skills. The process is very useful, in Esther O'Halloran's view, as it begins to build the team spirit considered so vital to Pret's culture.

CASE STUDY

GCHQ selects specialist staff

Government Communications HQ (GCHQ) employs around 4,000 staff, who study international communications for intelligence purposes and protect UK communications from hostile attack. GCHQ recruits between 200 and 300 people annually to its civil service operation. This involves running up to 30 different recruitment campaigns that could take on between one and 60 employees in any one round.

Recruitment at GCHQ is governed by the Civil Service Commissioners' "free, fair and open competition" code, which promotes equality of opportunity. All vacant posts are widely advertised to encourage applications from a broad range of people.

Assessment centres are the preferred selection method for around 40% of new employees and are used at two levels: for graduate-level recruitment (which includes candidates who may not have a degree but have compensatory work experience), and for internal promotion to some management grades.

Head of recruitment Geoff Trett explains GCHQ's approach to graduate-level recruitment: "Our external recruitment programme reflects the high intellectual and skills base needed for operations at GCHQ. Our main two assessment centres are therefore used for our technical campaigns and to select intelligence analysts."

The technical campaign

The assessment centre for graduate-level entry to a technical post at GCHQ is a 24-hour event and includes an overnight stay. The venue is a local Cheltenham hotel, where eight candidates assemble at 3pm to embark on a series of tests. The first challenge is a psychometric questionnaire involving numerical and written exercises. An opportunity to relax and socialise follows, with a senior technical representative of the company arriving for dinner and an informal chat.

The next day, the assessment process begins in earnest with one-to-one interviews for all candidates, conducted by HR and technical specialists. These are followed by a group exercise where would-be recruits are presented with a problem-solving scenario. The final hurdle is a psychological test that involves a self-assessment questionnaire and an interview with a psychologist. The group is released at 3pm, when the whole process starts again for the next set of hopefuls.

As GCHQ operates a rolling recruitment programme for technical posts, each assessment centre is likely to be repeated several times over a period of two or three weeks. This means that as many as 240 candidates could be assessed for around 50 to 60 posts, making it "a major logistical exercise". However, as Geoff Trett points out, a carefully planned matrix with clearly allocated responsibilities for administrative tasks helps the process to run smoothly. The event takes place three or four times a year.

A pool of specially trained assessors, drawn from relevant areas of the organisation, is available to assist on the day. The ratio is five assessors to eight candidates, made up of two technical assessors, two HR representatives and one psychologist. Though there is some variation in the precise make-up of the team on a day-to-day basis due to the intensity of the programme, it is felt that continuity is vital in order to preserve fairness. To achieve this, the organisers ensure that at least some assessors are "carried over" to the next day.

Variation on a theme

The assessment centre process used to select intelligence analysts is a shorter event and starts at 8.30am with a lunchtime finish. As relatively few intelligence analysts are taken on by the organisation, assessment centres are organised on an ad-hoc basis. Six people attend at any one time, and the event is held at the GCHQ offices.

The process begins with two written tests, both of which are job-related. The first one is a "sizeable analytical exercise" that involves assimilating a significant amount of information, drawing conclusions and writing up the results. The second exercise requires the candidate to advise on a specific course of action following consideration of related data. A one-to-one interview follows.

The final selection test is a group exercise, with candidates presented with a logistical problem to solve. A number of possible solutions are offered and the group is invited to reach a consensus on the most suitable one. As Geoff Trett explains: "We are not just looking for who steers and directs the group. We are also observing how candidates contribute in other positive ways, for example, by facilitating the discussion."

A competency-based approach

GCHQ's competency framework is the bedrock of its selection process. It consists of 14 competencies, although the organisation has plans to reduce these to seven. They include:

- communication;

- customer focus;

- delivering results;

- gaining cooperation and influence;

- IT knowledge;

- specialist or technical knowledge; and

- staff management.

Five or six key competencies are chosen that are considered vital to a particular role and evidence of these is carefully assessed at the assessment centre.

A means to an end

In Geoff Trett's view, using assessment centres for some employee groups delivers value for money and yields high-validity results. However, he does not believe that they would be an effective selection method for all staff: "Assessment centres are very good at producing all-rounders, but could run the risk of not recognising some rare and specialist skills. For example, we employ some of the most brilliant mathematicians in the country, who excel in their field but may not perform so outstandingly in a group."

Sources

1. Assessment centres, Association of Graduate Recruiters, 2001, www.agr.org.uk, price £15 (free to AGR members).

2. Redefining the fast stream, Cabinet Office, September 2001, www.civil-service.gov.uk.

3. "Assess your staff with a modern business plan", Widget Finn, *The Times*, 18 January 2001.

Chapter 13
Employer references

The death of references has been confidently expected for many years. Until recently, the practice of laboriously following up testimonials was seen as an anachronism – a throwback to the "characters" that decided the fate of servants in Victorian times. But latterly, high-profile scandals involving the recruitment of dishonest, incompetent or homicidal employees have led to the passage of legislation designed to protect the public and action being taken by a wide range of employers.

This chapter covers the main issues involved in the use of references, including when and how references are obtained, the information sought, the outcomes of the process and the main points of the law. It then looks at how employers respond when they are asked to provide a reference. Much of the information here is based on a survey of 113 employers carried out by IRS[1], but it is supplemented by extensive case studies, together presenting a detailed picture of employer practices.

THE CASE FOR REFERENCES

- They allow employers to check on information provided by potential employees.
- They involve little cost or relatively little effort.
- Many employers have found them useful, and they do influence appointment decisions.

THE CASE AGAINST REFERENCES

- The law on what must, may and may not be revealed is complex and difficult to apply.
- A discrepancy between what is said by a candidate and what is said by a referee may reflect unfairly on the candidate's version of events.
- Candidates may be reluctant to allow recruiters to approach their current employer until they have secured a job offer.

HOW COMMON ARE CHECKS ON REFERENCES?

Reference-checking is one of employers' most widely practised recruitment methods, after interviews, application forms and CVs, according to the Chartered Institute of

Personnel and Development[2]. In all, just under three-quarters of employers (73%) use references in their appointment decisions, although there is a sharp divide between private and public sector practices. While only seven in 10 private sector firms use them, this rises to almost nine in 10 public sector bodies.

Few users confine reference-checking to particular vacancies or candidates, though. The IRS study found that eight out of ten organisations that take up references have a simple, uniform policy of reference-checking across the board, leaving just one-sixth that are selective. Smaller employers are as likely to follow a universal approach as larger organisations and manufacturers that use references are comparatively less likely to have a policy of following up references for each and every vacancy or candidate.

Where an organisation does not always take up a reference, most commonly, the level of the vacancy acts as a trigger. A few employers make random checks, while others follow a variety of other approaches, such as obtaining references for permanent appointments, but not for fixed-term or temporary workers.

GETTING THE MOST OUT OF REFERENCES

When should you take them up?

References typically occupy the final stage in the lengthy process of filling a vacancy. A decision is usually made on a favoured candidate, and he or she is offered appointment "subject to satisfactory references". Seven in 10 employers wait until this point before they follow up references.

Fewer than a quarter obtain references at the stage before this: when interviews have been completed, but before the choice of candidate has been made. Finally, one in 14 employers conduct their reference checks even earlier in the process, before interviews take place.

Smaller employers are even more likely to leave reference-checking until the end of the selection process. Conversely, the public sector places much greater weight on following up references earlier in the process. Most commonly, public sector employers obtain references after the final interview, but prior to the selection decision.

Decisions about the timing of reference checks will partly be influenced by the importance attached to the information obtained from referees. Where references are given a narrow role of merely confirming basic factual details, then it may be appropriate to delay their use until after a job offer has been made.

Some employers argue that by taking up references at an early stage they can try to resolve conflicting information from candidates and their former employers.

Should they be in writing?

Employers overwhelmingly prefer formal references, making their requests in writing (or by email) and receiving the reference via the same medium. There is little indication of a switch to using the telephone or face-to-face interviews to obtain references, despite many employers' perceptions that written references are becoming less informative.

More than three-quarters of employers IRS contacted always obtain written references (by letter or email), and a further one-fifth do so on occasion. In other words, less than 1% of employers never use written or emailed references, but rely on verbal ones.

So, for the vast majority of organisations using references in recruitment, the telephone is merely a fallback. When there is no response to a reference request, or when time is short, a referee may be contacted by telephone. Often, though, the employers involved told us that they would then also ask for the details to be confirmed in writing.

More than eight in 10 employers that use written references also make use of a reference questionnaire or form that they send to the referees.

How do you assess a reference

Weighing up the information that referees supply is rarely an easy task, even where some form or structure is provided. In many cases, though, a reference is seen as a simple safety net against flagrant deceptions on the part of the candidate, rather than contributing in a fuller way to the appointment decision.

Potentially, though, a reference can provide information and feedback on a wide range of issues relating to the candidate. It can confirm, or disclose for the first time, the candidate's current salary, for example, and verify basic details such as the person's job title and employment dates.

Most employers are interested in a range of factors, as the table below shows. Many employers have formulated a policy on what can and cannot be included in the references supplied to others - usually, to prevent the expression of opinions and other non-factual information. But even such employers are ready to seek, and use, such feedback when they are in the position of obtaining references from others. More than three-quarters of employers with a reference-giving policy are still interested in referees' opinions of candidates' performance, and almost two-thirds continue to be interested in referees' opinions about candidates' suitability for the vacancies being filled. Employers without policies limiting the content of references they supply are even less inhibited.

Figure 2: Areas of interest in references

Absence record	89.3%
Opinion of candidate's performance	83.9%
Opinion of candidate's suitability for vacancy	69.6%
Work history	65.2%
Punctuality	63.4%
Disciplinary record	61.6%
Responsibilities of current job	54.5%
Motivation/commitment	50.9%
Gaps found in CV/application form	28.6%
Current salary	25.0%
Qualifications	21.4%
Criminal convictions	13.4%
Creditworthiness	7.1%
Reason for leaving*	6.2%
Membership of professional etc body	5.4%
Honesty/integrity*	4.5%
Whether would re-employ*	3.6%

* While the other areas in the table were based on a list we supplied, these three topics were volunteered by respondents, and this may underrepresent their prevalence.

BEYOND THE REFERENCE

References are just one of the means at employers' disposal to check the *bona fides* of job applicants.

For sensitive posts, such as working with children, there is a vetting system in place where employers can obtain disclosures from the Criminal Records Bureau (which replaced the system of police checks). And, where relevant, employers can have applicants checked against lists of unsuitable people, which are maintained by government departments. For financial posts of a sensitive nature, credit-reference agencies are also available.

The standard of checking and vetting for sensitive posts has been driven up in recent years, partly because of self-regulation and government legislation intended to remedy weaknesses exposed by several high-profile instances where unqualified or dangerous individuals gained employment through falsified applications.

But, more generally, employers may be concerned about conducting reference and other checks because of perceptions that inaccurate or downright deceitful job applications are increasingly common.

According to the Risk Advisory Group, for example, lies and inaccuracies rose by more than 20% in a sample of 877 of the CVs that it checked on behalf of client employers during the final quarter of 2001. In all, it says it found that 54% of these CVs "showed some form of discrepancy". However, as many such surveys show, it adds that "most of these discrepancies are harmless omissions or honest mistakes, and need not affect the hiring decision".

There are now several agencies, such as the Risk Advisory Group, Experian, the Control Risks Group and CV Validation, that offer services linked to the verification of candidates' details. These range from obtaining standard references, to qualification checking (Experian has an arrangement with British higher education institutions that it claims speeds up the process of confirming academic qualifications), credit checks and verifying home addresses. Details of bankruptcies, present and past directorships, media coverage of the person, membership of professional bodies, and confirming dates of birth are also on offer. Ethical agencies always require the candidate's prior permission for such checks and some share the results of their searches with the individual.

DO REFERENCES MAKE A DIFFERENCE?

The IRS study found that six out of ten employers had rejected at least one candidate or had failed to confirm a provisional offer of employment in the previous year as a direct result of what was said in a reference. In a quarter of cases, references had led to the rejection of at least three candidates over the year, with one in ten organisations rejecting five or more people.

And, importantly, employers with sensitive posts – such as work with children and vulnerable adults, or in financial services – are proportionately more likely to reject applicants because of their use of references than employers as a whole.

A NOTE ON THE LAW

The law relating to references has developed piecemeal, from court decisions and from Acts of Parliament focusing on addressing abuses in particular occupations and industries. The lack of a single or prime source of legislation has probably heightened the impact of a number of legal cases in recent years.

In general, there is no legal obligation for an employer to provide a reference in respect of a current or former employee, unless required to do so under a contract of employment or other agreement. There may also be special considerations where occupations or industries are regulated, such as financial services.

Discrimination claims

A refusal to supply a reference to a current employee who has complained of discrimination, however, might be interpreted as victimisation under one of the discrimination statutes.

Nevertheless, a recent House of Lords judgment (*Chief Constable of West Yorkshire Police v Khan*) permits courts to consider the reasons for the refusal to supply a reference. In Khan, the House of Lords found that the reason related to the employer's current defence of a discrimination complaint, and not to a desire to victimise the individual.

In respect of former employees, refusal to provide a reference may constitute victimisation under the Sex Discrimination Act 1975, and the government has already signalled its intention to extend this principle to all areas of discrimination covered by the Race Directive and the Equal Treatment in Employment Directive. Implementation will take place in stages between 2003 and 2006.

Negligence

Where a reference is supplied, the employer and person writing it have a common-law duty of care to both the subject of the reference and its recipient. The duty involves ensuring that the reference is accurate and fair – both in terms of what the reference says, and any significant details that are left out – and a claim for negligence might arise where the duty of care has not been met.

The famous case of *Spring v Guardian Assurance* involved a claim against Mr Spring's former employer, Guardian Assurance, which reached the House of Lords. His reference was so damning that it was described as the "kiss of death", and he failed to gain the reregistration with the relevant financial services regulatory body that would enable him to continue his career. While a claim of malicious falsehood (defamation) failed, he succeeded in a claim of negligence. It was found that the employer had not checked its facts, and had made unsubstantiated allegations. The case established that the duty of care covers not only the person receiving a reference, but also the individual who is the subject of it.

On the other hand, the temptation to omit any controversial or critical information from a reference may also lead to a breach of the law. References do not have to be comprehensive, but should not give a misleading impression when their recipients read them, whether this is due to the inclusion of inaccurate information or to the omission of important facts.

Defamation – libel and slander – in respect of false information in references is more difficult to prove. The concept of "qualified privilege" enables referees to claim that they believed the statements to be true, while the individual faces the difficult task of proving that the referee acted with malice.

Mutual trust

As well as the common-law duty of care, references are also subject to the concept of the implied term of mutual trust and confidence that the law considers to form part of every contract of employment. In another well-known case, *TSB Bank plc v Harris*, the bank supplied a reference that revealed several complaints about Ms Harris of which she herself was unaware. The complaints might or might not have been factually correct, but the Employment Appeal Tribunal ruled that "simply to be accurate in what is said may not lead to a 'reasonable and fair' reference".

As well as potential negligence claims from new employers or former employees, employers supplying references for current employees that do not follow the above principles may be subject to a claim of constructive dismissal if the employee resigns as a result.

Unsatisfactory references

Job offers are legally binding contracts, and they cannot usually be withdrawn simply because a reference contains information that changes the recruiters' decision about the appointment – unless it reveals that the candidate has lied. To do so might leave the employer open to a claim for breach of contract – that is, earnings lost during the applicable notice period. To avoid this, it is common practice to offer employment on a conditional basis – "subject to satisfactory references". In *Wishart v NACAB*, the Court of Appeal considered that "satisfactory" meant only that the employer must consider the reference in good faith.

Data protection

References that employers receive about job applicants are covered by the Data Protection Act 1998. Although it is commonly believed that the Act gives individuals the right to gain access to references about them, in fact, they are explicitly excluded from access requirements (under Schedule 7 of the Act) – unless the reference was not given in confidence. However, like any other document, a court can order the disclosure of a reference where it may be relevant to a case before it.

However, two recent publications from the Office of the Information Commissioner[3] limit the Act's exemption, by applying it solely while a confidential reference is "in the hands of the organisation which gave it". Once the reference has been received by the intended recipient, these publications say that the exemption does not apply. There would, though, be a breach of the referee's own rights if their identity were to be revealed without consent, and the Code says that "the recipient is entitled to take steps to withhold information that reveals the identity of other individuals, such as the author of the reference".

Regulated employment

Just as there is no general obligation on employers to provide references, there is no universal requirement to obtain references in respect of people applying to work with an organisation. However, some occupations and industries are covered by legislation designed to protect the public from unqualified or dangerous workers, where reference-checking is a legal requirement.

Independent hospitals, clinics and medical agencies, for example, are covered by the Care Standards Act 2000. The Department of Health has issued a number of National Minimum Standards under this Act, which are to be taken into account by the National Care Standards Commission when ascertaining whether or not an independent healthcare employer is registered with it and, therefore, can continue in business.

CHECKLIST

Key points to remember

- **Put the admin in place:** tell candidates what will be required and when, and make sure it is someone's job to administer reference checks and follow up late responses.

- **Decide when to take up references:** do it early and you will be better able to act on what you are told; do it late and there is less work and less chance of deterring candidates whose current employers don't know they are looking for a new job.

- **Choose who should provide a reference:** they should have recent first-hand knowledge of the candidate or be able to verify factual information provided by the candidate.

- **Decide on a structure:** many researchers believe referees provide more comprehensive replies when asked to follow a set format such as a questionnaire.

- **Decide whether to go for verbal or written references:** a referee may be more candidate if they do not have to commit their thoughts to paper, but may provide a more thoughtful and thorough view in writing.

- **Choose what background information to provide the referee:** the more they know about the post and the skills, experience and qualifications you are looking for, the more they should be able to help.

- **Take a reality check:** referees are not necessarily more accurate or unbiased than job applicants. If in doubt, go back to the referee for more information or ask the candidate to explain any discrepancy.

CASE STUDY

National Portrait Gallery acts early on

The National Portrait Gallery employs around 180 staff, ranging from curators to retail assistants, and from managers to support staff. The gallery checks references for all potential recruits and asks job candidates to supply details of three referees on its standard application form. Candidates are invited to tick a box indicating whether references can be obtained prior to interview. "In the majority of cases, we are able to take up references before the interview process," says Caroline Wynter, personnel manager. "The job circuit for galleries and museums is quite a small one, and jobhunters are likely to have already approached their managers to gain support for a career move."

The process for requesting references is carried out in tandem with inviting candidates for interview. A structured form, together with a copy of the job description and person specification, is sent out to referees. Factual information, such as job tenure, reason for leaving and attendance record is requested on the candidate, as well as the referee's opinion on the candidate's suitability for the vacancy. Caroline Wynter reports that employers are generally forthcoming when providing comments on suitability for the post, which she attributes in part to the more transparent process that is encouraged by seeking references up front. She explains: "When job applicants are asked to allow referees to be contacted at an early stage, this may prompt people to discuss their application with their managers."

If the recruitment process reaches the stage where, following interview, no references have been received for the most suitable candidate, a conditional job offer can be made.

The gallery makes every effort to obtain all three references, but, at the very least, aims to gain feedback on a person's employment history for the past five years. Referees are given the option to return references by post, fax or email in a bid to speed up the process.

Because of the potential for physical loss from the collection, and some staff having access to children, security checks on all staff are carried out using the services of government agencies. These checks include criminal convictions and childcare lists. Caroline Wynter finds the service very effective, but lengthy. She says: "As it takes some time for clearance to be obtained, our offer letter clearly states that the job offer is conditional on acceptable checks having been made."

The gallery uses the telephone to follow up or clarify any information that is provided in writing, but prefers to receive written references. "Referees are definitely more forthcoming on the telephone, but people have to think more carefully about the information they are providing if giving a written reference," she says. Line managers have authority to provide references on current or former employees, but they must be copied to the personnel department. The gallery's employee handbook provides guidance on reference writing and stipulates that the reference should contain factual information only. "Managers are made aware that, when providing references, they are representing the views of the National Portrait Gallery," explains Caroline Wynter. "In view of recent legal precedents, care has to be exercised in the type of information disclosed."

When asked about the reliability and validity of references, Caroline Wynter states that their effectiveness varies in relation to their content. She says: "References are an important part of the selection jigsaw and are very helpful for verifying factual details, but they cannot be considered in isolation. A reference can confirm the view of a candidate that is formed during the selection process."

CASE STUDY

Hanover Housing Association uses structured forms

Hanover Housing Association provides sheltered accommodation for the elderly. The organisation has around 600 employees, nearly half of whom are estate managers on sheltered housing schemes for the elderly.

References are taken up for all job candidates, following final interview. If the housing association has reached a selection decision, a letter will be sent to the favourite candidate indicating an intention to offer them the job. Following the receipt of satisfactory references, the HR department writes again, confirming the conditional offer of appointment and enclosing a copy of the contract.

The housing association always obtains written references on potential recruits by sending referees a structured form covering the following areas:

- position held and salary;
- honesty and capability;
- reliability;
- ability to get on with others;
- ability to work well under pressure;
- absence record, including significant periods of absence;
- details of any disciplinary action;
- whether or not the referee would re-employ the person;
- any reason why Hanover Housing Association should not employ the person; and
- additional information that the referee can provide if they wish.

If there is a need to appoint someone as quickly as possible, line managers initially assume responsibility for collecting references over the telephone. But, as recruitment manager Christine Armstrong explains: "If a referee is interviewed by phone, a generic script ensures that we collect identical information to that which is provided in the structured form." The recruitment team then follows this up by asking referees to complete the written form.

The housing association has rejected several potentially suitable candidates because of unfavourable references. One recent example involved a reference that indicated a lack of flexibility on the candidate's part. "We always follow up negative information, or any blanks in the data provided, very carefully," explains Christine Armstrong. "In this case, there was a strong requirement for flexibility in the post and, having discussed the issue with the recruiting manager, it was decided not to appoint the person." In such circumstances, the HR department writes to the candidate, explaining that the references have failed to meet all the necessary criteria.

The housing association is happy in principle to supply references for current or former employees that contain the same type of information that it expects to receive from referees. However, in view of the growing body of case law on references, limitations are placed on the extent of information given out. "Only personnel specialists have the authority to write references, and there are specific restrictions on what they contain," explains Christine Armstrong. "For instance, when providing details of someone's sickness absence history, we indicate only the number of absent days."

CASE STUDY

Portsmouth Education Department's detailed policy

Portsmouth Education Department employs around 5,000 people. Although teachers are recruited directly by schools in the city, recruitment is undertaken centrally for headteachers and support staff, such as advisers and educational psychologists.

The department follows the written reference-checking policy that applies across Portsmouth City Council. The policy runs to three pages and provides detailed guidance on areas such as providing references following disciplinary investigation or dismissal, and the disclosure of references. The document extract encapsulates the council's guiding principles. The policy is communicated to line managers and serves as an important guideline for all those involved in the recruitment process.

The department is rigorous when checking candidates' references: all references are checked, preferably prior to interview. As personnel and training manager Jacqueline Coonie explains: "We request permission to take up references when we invite job applicants for interview. If they decline, we ask them again when they attend for interview but we make it very clear that we will not make a job offer until we have checked references."

She reports that most candidates are happy for their referees to be contacted in advance. A significant number of prospective employees selected by the education department will be working with children. Although it is considered vitally important that proper checks are carried out on such candidates, the department consistently applies the same approach to all job candidates, irrespective of the type of vacancy.

The department takes up three references for headteacher posts and two for all other vacancies. The policy dictates that at least one referee must be the candidate's most recent employer and, preferably, all references should bear testament to the person's ability to perform the job in question. Although the department has occasionally obtained a reference by telephone if necessary, it is not the preferred choice. "If we are running out of time, we will contact a referee by telephone, but we always request that any information supplied on a candidate is backed up in writing," says Jacqueline Coonie. A structured letter is sent to all referees, requesting information on the following areas:

- work history;

- responsibilities of current or most recent job;

- absence record;

- punctuality;

- disciplinary record;

- motivation and commitment;

- the referee's opinion of the candidate's performance; and

- views on the candidate's suitability for the vacancy.

The education department does not place any restrictions on the type of information that is supplied to recruiting organisations on current or former employees. "We are very aware of the growing body of case law on references, but we believe it is important to be as helpful as possible to other organisations by providing a full reference," explains Jacqueline Coonie.

Although line managers and personnel specialists have the authority to supply information on areas such as conduct and suitability for the vacancy, no specific details are disclosed to third parties. Managers are also aware that, where issues relating to performance or conduct are provided in a reference, the subject of that reference must be made aware of the disclosure.

Jacqueline Coonie believes that reference-checking plays an important role in the selection process. "References are a very useful selection tool, but only in the context of the overall process," she says. The department has never rejected someone on the sole basis of a bad reference. In Jacqueline Coonie's view, if a negative testimonial is received, the candidate's unsuitability for the post is usually borne out by the whole selection process and there is no need to rely on the reference alone. She has noticed that, in the light of increasing legal liability, referees are more guarded in the information they supply on current or former employees.

Sources

1. "References: the check's in the post", *IRS Employment Review* 752, May 2002; "Of good character: supplying references and providing access", *IRS Employment Review* 754, June 2002.

2. Recruitment and retention survey 2002, Chartered Institute of Personnel and Development, www.cipd.co.uk.

3. The Data Protection Act: legal guidance, December 2001, and the Employment practices data protection Code, part one, March 2002; both published by the Office of the Information Commissioner, www.dataprotection.gov.uk.

Employer references

Chapter 14
Case study – Tesco Pharmacy

Tesco is the country's largest food retailer, with around 700 stores in the UK. The company established its first in-store Tesco Pharmacy in 1991 and, in the space of just over a decade, this has grown into a nationwide chain of 211 outlets.

The majority of the pharmacies are situated in the company's superstores and larger supermarkets known as "Tesco Extras", these retail outlets having the largest space available for non-food items.

Tesco Pharmacy is not operated as a separate business, but forms an integral part of Tesco's in-store health and beauty service. As Carol Trower, Tesco Pharmacy's recruitment and training manager, explains: "Our pharmacies are a pivotal part of health and beauty, helping to drive the sales in this area. We have therefore tried to establish pharmacies in all our big retail outlets, although obtaining the necessary NHS contract for each individual store is a long and difficult process."

Around 360 pharmacy managers and pharmacists are employed by Tesco, together with a core team of specialist staff to run a pharmacy outlet. Each pharmacy typically needs a complement of one pharmacy manager, two or three full-time-equivalent pharmacists, a trained dispenser and around 10 trained assistants.

Continuous training and development is an integral and necessary part of resourcing the pharmacies. Dispensers are trained to at least NVQ Level 3. Pharmacy assistants are drawn from the in-store employee population, but they first have to undergo a comprehensive training programme.

Filling vacancies for these groups of staff, although representing a busy recruitment activity, does not pose a serious challenge. But the same cannot be said of recruiting to pharmacy manager and pharmacist posts. "There is fierce competition for pharmacists, and in the past five or six years the problem has worsened in the industry," comments Trower.

LINKS WITH UNIVERSITIES

Only 16 universities provide relevant pharmacy courses, with some 1,600 pharmacists graduating each year. The job opportunities open to them are many and varied.

Whereas a decade ago, most newly qualified pharmacists would follow a traditional career path, there are now an increasing number of options open to them, such as being attached to a GP surgery as a primary care pharmacist, becoming a locum pharmacist or moving into other professions altogether.

As an illustration of the last point, Trower herself is a pharmacist, but moved into the human resources field by building on the communication and people-management skills that are vital to a pharmacist's role.

"Pharmacy starts off as a general science degree, which opens up all sorts of other opportunities and, combined with the insufficient numbers graduating each year, there are simply not enough pharmacists to go round," she says.

In a move that made a difficult situation even worse, the three-year pharmacy course was changed to a four-year Masters in 1997. This switch meant that no new pharmacy graduates were available for employment in 2001.

Tesco Pharmacy has a well-established long-term recruitment strategy to meet its staffing needs. A key part of its approach is maintaining strong links with the universities that run the pharmacy courses. Tesco Pharmacy employees have a direct presence in five of these institutions, spending half their working week lecturing to students. The company also liaises extensively with the other 11 universities, as Trower points out: "There is an 18-month recruitment process: it begins in February for penultimate-year students with careers talks and presentations, and we interview in September for recruitment the following summer."

MYTHS ABOUT HIGH STREET PHARMACY

Tesco Pharmacy has also had to develop a strategy to meet more immediate and pressing recruitment needs. At present, the company has a vacancy rate for pharmacists that, although not unusual for the industry, means it has an ambitious target of recruiting 135 new pharmacists. "We are already well on the way to achieving our goal," says Trower. "Our recruitment ability has improved tremendously compared with a few years ago, so I am optimistic about reaching our target."

Generally, though, the pharmacy sector in the UK suffers from acute recruitment difficulties, which led the company to embark on an extensive research programme in 1998.

The study examined pharmacists' career choices and explored their views on working for a big retail company such as Tesco, compared with a more traditional high-street pharmacy. Focus groups were held in-house as well as externally with groups of pharmacists working in other businesses.

The results of the research were illuminating, especially from those outside the company, and have served to inform Tesco's recruitment advertising campaigns ever since.

"We had very encouraging feedback from our own employees on what Tesco is like as an employer," says Trower. "The comments from other pharmacists focused on why they had reservations about working for a big retailer. There was concern that Tesco's pharmacies were not 'proper' pharmacies, had a 'checkout culture' and could not provide the same level of service as a high-street outlet."

HOW THE COMPANY RESPONDED

The company's response to the research was to develop a recruitment strategy that emphasised its similarities with high-street pharmacies, while promoting the distinctive advantages of working for a supportive and flexible employer. For example, one advertising campaign focused on getting the message across that Tesco's dispensaries attract exactly the same range of customers as their high-street counterparts, be they pensioners or mothers with sick children needing a prescription in the middle of the night. The last scenario, which featured as an image in one advertisement, also promoted the service that the stores can provide through their longer opening hours.

Another campaign concentrated on the flexibility that Tesco Pharmacy employees can enjoy. Staff can work full time or part time, across a variety of different shift patterns, and full-timers can have the choice of a 36-, 39- or 42-hour week.

"Flexible working is an integral part of Tesco's culture and a key recruitment and retention tool," explains Trower. "For example, career breaks of up to five years can be taken by staff and mean that our newly qualified pharmacists can travel the world and come back to work for us."

Another series of recruitment advertisements linked the topic of flexible working with the use of medical imagery. One advert featured a man imprisoned in a pill bottle with the caption: "We like to give our pharmacists as much freedom as possible".

WINNING JOB ADVERTISEMENTS

The key focus of Tesco Pharmacy's recruitment is its powerful advertising campaigns, and it is these that generate the overwhelming majority of applications from pharmacists. Trower estimates that each full-page colour advertisement generates at least 50 phone calls, with the smaller ads prompting around 20 enquiries. Since it outsourced its recruitment advertising to resourcing specialist Bernard Hodes in 1996, the two companies have scooped nine Chartered Institute of Personnel and Development and RADS (Recruitment Advertising) awards and nominations.

Trower describes Tesco Pharmacy's outsourcing arrangement with Bernard Hodes as "a very good working relationship". The company has worked with the same account handler since the start, which, in her view, has helped the consultancy to develop a keen understanding of what is needed.

Every campaign involves close collaboration between Trower and Bernard Hodes, with every detail of the artwork and wording of the designs being agreed before production. "We have worked with Bernard Hodes on at least six campaigns now, most of them back-to-back, and it has definitely been cost-effective for our recruitment," she says. "The BH people are very proactive and always come up with fresh, eye-catching ideas."

However, to ensure that the company was receiving the best value for money, Tesco Pharmacy put its most recent advertising campaign out to tender but, as Trower comments, "Bernard Hodes still produced the winning designs."

TARGETING THE RIGHT AUDIENCE

Each recruitment advertising campaign runs for several months and is built around a clearly defined concept. The full-page adverts that lead the campaign are placed only in the *Pharmaceutical Journal*, the professional magazine that all pharmacists registered with the Royal Pharmaceutical Society receive as part of their membership. These powerful and colourful poster images are followed up by regular quarter-page advertisements promoting specific regional vacancies.

The theme for the one recent advertising initiative is "fairytales", and all the leading advertisements feature a well-known childhood story with which everyone can immediately identify.

EMPLOYER REPUTATION

Trower believes that, while the company's distinctive advertising approach serves as a powerful recruitment tool, it is Tesco's reputation as an employer that is instrumental in recruiting and retaining staff.

"We are very serious about what we do at Tesco Pharmacy," she says. "Pharmacists are accountable for their activities to their professional body, and we try to project a highly professional image to support that responsibility."

Training and development are an integral part of the company's people-management approach, and this is emphasised in all recruitment advertising literature. It will soon be mandatory for pharmacists to undertake at least 30 hours' continuing professional development each year. To support them in fulfilling this requirement, Tesco Pharmacy has developed a training portfolio for all its pharmacists that enables them to record their development activities and complete the necessary forms.

Succession and career planning are also considered vital to both the development of staff and ensuring continuity in the business. There is a clearly defined career path for pharmacists and the opportunity is there for a pharmacist to progress to a pharmacy manager role after a year's employment. Beyond that, there are six regional pharmacy manager roles based in key locations across the country, providing considerable responsibilities for staff support in the pharmacy operation.

Tesco Pharmacy believes that it is important to offer competitive salary and benefits packages to attract high-quality recruits. A newly qualified pharmacist can expect an annual salary of around £32,000, more than double the earnings of a trainee and "more generous than what is offered by many high-street pharmacies", according to Trower. There is also scope for salary progression in the pharmacy pay bands plus a store-wide profit-share scheme, which this year saw Tesco employees enjoying a share of £48 million.

"We look after our employees at Tesco, and our retention rates are very good," comments Trower. "If we do lose staff, it is usually within the first six months because they have decided the career or the company are not for them."

REGIONAL RECRUITMENT

The selection of pharmacists is a core part of each regional pharmacy manager's role and, collectively, they undertake 16 days of interviewing a month. Initial applications are screened centrally and, if considered suitable, interview dates are scheduled as part of a rolling recruitment programme that is planned well in advance. The appointment ratio is high, with around two in three suitable candidates accepting job offers.

Induction is also an important part of the recruitment process and a newly appointed pharmacist spends two weeks (four weeks for a pharmacy manager) shadowing an approved trainer. "We induct our new staff very thoroughly," says Trower. "It is important that pharmacists who are new to the company spend as much time as possible getting to know every part of the business, and our mentor approach allows them to do that."

At the end of the process, all new pharmacists have to be validated by the regional pharmacy manager and the induction period is extended, if necessary.

EXPLORING NEW AVENUES

Tesco Pharmacy is not afraid to test new techniques to attract potential recruits. For example, in February 2002 the company started to develop an online recruitment portal.

"We are still at the early stages of building a web presence to attract applicants, but already there have been some success stories with hard-to-fill vacancies," Trower says. There is no online application form available as yet, but she believes that this is a priority for the future.

"Our website generates a lot of interest, but because non-pharmacist candidates can submit either an application form or a CV, a high proportion of applications are unsuitable," she explains. "An application form could stipulate the necessary pharmacy qualifications and filter out unsuitable applications."

Another recent experiment is the use of a search consultancy, Resourcing, to help fill long-term vacancies. The contract with Resourcing is tightly managed and the agency works to a very specific brief.

Each vacancy is dealt with on an individual basis and, in view of the costs involved in this type of activity, is passed on to the consultancy to deal with only as a last resort. "We engaged the agency eight weeks ago and interviewed the first candidate last week, so we are keeping the service under review for now," Trower told us when we interviewed her in early July. She pointed out that Tesco Pharmacy carefully researched the agency before engaging its headhunting services.

FEEDBACK AND REVIEW

Tesco Pharmacy is constantly reviewing and evaluating its recruitment and selection processes to ensure that the company maximises their effectiveness. Regular focus groups are still convened in-house to sound out employees on a range of employment and business issues. One method the company uses to measure its recruitment activities is gathering feedback from candidates who requested an application form but did not return it.

"Evaluation of our recruitment procedures is fundamental, and so we send out questionnaires with a prepaid envelope," says Trower. "This approach has paid dividends and the comments we receive are invaluable."

The survey form asks for applicants' perceptions of the recruitment process, and questions include: "How was your initial enquiry handled?" and "Why did you not complete the application form?" Around 30% of those surveyed return completed questionnaires and, on occasion, the practice has even led to renewed career interest in Tesco Pharmacy.

The company is quick to act on the results of the evaluation exercise and, for example, speeded up the application process following feedback that it was too slow. As Trower concludes: "It is a tough recruitment market out there and we aim to seize every opportunity to live up to Tesco's values."

Chapter 15
Case study – B&Q

Over recent years, home improvement chain B&Q has undergone a massive expansion programme as it worked towards its target of having 175 Warehouse stores in the UK by the end of 2003. By 2001 it had opened 60 new retail outlets, and had plans to open another 25 every year after that. This creates an ambitious agenda for a recruitment programme, demanding 14,000 new staff each year, alongside finding replacements for normal wastage.

The company, part of the Kingfisher group, has won several accolades, including Retailer of the Year 1999 and, in 2000, *Retail Week*'s Retail Employer of the Year award, based on satisfaction indicators such as customer service and employee attitudes.

THE CHALLENGE

An expansion plan on this scale has enormous implications for a company's recruitment and retention strategy. As Sonia Reeves, resourcing manager with B&Q, comments: "B&Q is growing at a phenomenal rate, and the challenge of resourcing new and existing stores is considerable." The company already employs 27,000 people.

In Reeves's view, the challenge is twofold. The first is to fill such a large volume of vacancies with people of the right calibre. Second, this must be achieved against a backdrop of relatively high employment.

"In many regions we are recruiting in the context of a tight labour market," says Reeves. "It is also the case that people are therefore more discerning about where they choose to work and how they want to live their lives generally."

In her view, this directly affects people's attitudes to the hours they are prepared to work, the expectation of a work–life balance and their mobility. The reputation of the retail sector, which is known for its low-pay culture, is an additional obstacle.

The majority of new posts are customer advisers, experts and checkout operators, although the company needs to recruit significant numbers to a variety of different management roles. "We know that our most successful stores are run by good managers, so recruiting experienced and talented people to our management roles is pivotal," says Reeves.

The company is creating both full-time and part-time positions. As trading hours are from 7am to 9pm in most stores, this provides opportunities for flexible working arrangements. As Reeves explains, "In line with B&Q's excellent record for diversity, we aim to match the requirements of the business with employees' individual needs, and so try to facilitate a range of different working patterns to suit, for instance, working mothers."

THE STRATEGY

There are a number of strands to B&Q's resourcing strategy. "Having recognised the challenge in the first place, we identified the stakeholders we need to work with to achieve our recruitment plan," says Reeves. As well as building strong working relationships with third parties, such as the advertising agency used by the company, this approach has much wider implications.

"We need to devise ways of attracting people to fit with our brand," says Reeves. "Most of our potential employees are our customers, so, first, we have to consider external perceptions of the brand. This means that if our people in the stores are not happy in their work, they will not attract potential employees." The resourcing strategy therefore begins at an internal level and means engaging employees' aspirations by marrying the opportunities for business growth with opportunities for people.

"The resourcing plan cannot operate in isolation," says Reeves. "It has to be strategic and take on board all aspects of the business." Human resource planning is considered integral to the process and this activity is both bottom-up and top-down.

"I have to link our resourcing needs with the development and requirements of the business in order to identify any gaps, which requires a very clear line of sight on what B&Q is trying to achieve," explains Reeves.

"On one level, it is a numbers game, as we will need about 250 to 300 new staff to open a new store." But equally important are the more local projections of other statistics, such as turnover and possible promotions. "Geographically, I can have an overview of where the hot spots are, taking into account business expansion and labour shortages, but the comprehensive information provided by the regions completes the picture," says Reeves.

She believes that only by coordinating both sets of data can a company as big as B&Q really achieve "value for money" in its long-term people planning. These numerous and complex sets of information are then translated into a "demand statement", which sets out the detailed labour requirements for each store.

Reeves believes that the compilation of a coherent resourcing plan is only made possible by the close relationship of B&Q's central HR team, its regional resourcing managers and the company's other business functions, such as marketing. "There has to be excellent communication channels in place throughout the business and the regions to make it work," says Reeves. "There also has be synergy in what these different areas of the business are trying to achieve. It means working as a team."

Although B&Q's resourcing strategy is a national one, regional recruitment activities may vary in response to local labour market conditions. Generally, the company experiences recruitment difficulties where there are the most acute labour shortages, such as London, the South East and the Channel Islands. Regional staff in such areas may organise more targeted recruitment campaigns by advertising or holding job fairs in local stores. A group of stores in an area may also join forces and arrange a regional recruitment fair in a local venue.

SUCCESSION AND CAREER PLANNING

The other important feature of B&Q's resourcing strategy is its succession and career planning. Reeves believes that the career opportunities offered by B&Q are unrivalled in the retail sector. "B&Q has a great story to tell about career progression," she says.

The vast majority of B&Q store managers have progressed through the business, bringing valuable on-the-job experience to the role. B&Q tries to fill about 70% of its managerial vacancies via internal promotion. A fast-track mechanism identifies high-calibre employees who have management potential, and the company's development centre then provides the springboard for technical and management training.

However, given the company's level of growth, there are simply not enough budding managers already working for B&Q to fuel the current expansion programme. "We also have to be careful not to promote people too quickly, before they are ready for such a responsible role," says Reeves. "We have to strike a balance, and also have a clear strategy of attracting external applications."

Hitherto, most of these external management appointments have involved people who are already experienced in the retail sector. However, B&Q plans to widen its recruitment net to attract people from other industries where recruits could bring valuable and transferable skills to the job.

TELEPHONE SCREENING

All external recruitment queries are handled by a central "recruitment response centre", which is based in Glasgow. A team of experienced staff deals with about 350,000 calls annually – a figure that makes B&Q's recruitment targets look easily achievable after all. The aims in setting up the centre were to manage a large volume of job applications in a cost-effective and efficient manner and to achieve consistency in the initial screening of candidates.

"We need to know for certain that the company is treating everyone equally in the recruitment process," says Reeves. "As well as wanting to have tighter control over the calibre of people we are taking on, we also want to give candidates a great experience."

The recruitment centre uses an automated telephone screening interview (ATSI) system for the preliminary screening process. This computerised selection tool was especially designed for B&Q by Gallup.

Job hopefuls are presented with a series of statements and asked to select numbers 1 to 5, which correspond to a scale ranging from "strongly agree" to "strongly disagree". Candidates must score a high percentage mark to progress to the next stage of the selection process. The questions are designed to assess whether or not candidates would be suited to the company, and focus on key areas such as attitude to work and customer service.

"From the results of this brief exercise, we gain an important feel for how customer- and delivery-oriented people are – two aspects that are considered essential to a good fit with the organisation," says Reeves. The interview questions were developed after an extensive number of interviews with some of B&Q's highest-performing employees. "In this way, we know that we are focusing on the key behavioural traits for building a successful 'can-do' business," says Reeves.

Interestingly, labour turnover at B&Q has dropped since introducing the screening tool. Reeves does not believe that it is possible to attribute improved retention rates solely to ATSI. However, she believes that assessing applicants' potential fit with the company culture at an early stage of the recruitment process addresses a key retention issue.

The company has received "very positive feedback" on ATSI from both successful and unsuccessful candidates when asked how effectively they were able to represent themselves. Store managers are also pleased with its results, reporting that the tool produces a very good pool of candidates.

Another advantage of the automated interview, in Reeves's view, is the guarantee that the process in non-discriminatory. "The only details given to recruiting managers are job-related," she explains. "There is no possibility of potential discrimination, as information relating to personal characteristics such as age, sex, race and disability are not displayed."

Those candidates who successfully complete the first selection hurdle are asked to complete an application form. Details from the forms are passed to stores but are restricted to data such as the candidate's skills and abilities. To further ensure that the process is non-discriminatory, personal characteristics are only passed to recruiters at the interview stage. Selection interviews are conducted on a one-to-one basis by store managers.

PEOPLE ARE THE TOOLS OF THE TRADE

B&Q places its employees – "customer-focused people who share our drive to be nothing but the best" – at the heart of its success. The company culture, which is described by Reeves as "informal, positive and very friendly," is thought to play a major role in retaining workers. "There is a great team spirit in all our stores," says Reeves. "The culture really respects the input of the individual and we endeavour to enable everyone to make the most of their particular talents."

The company's commitment to valuing the contribution that individual employees can make to the business is reflected in its diversity strategy. "Everyone has a unique set of skills and experience," says Reeves. "That diversity of background and knowledge is an integral part of the success of any business."

B&Q has a long and impressive record on diversity, having won numerous awards in this field. Its strategies and policies in areas such as disability and employing older workers are also considered integral to both recruiting and retaining staff.

Although one of B&Q's original goals in the 1980s was to tap into alternative pools of labour, its employment strategy to develop a diverse workforce now has a much wider aim. "We want to reflect the local communities in which our stores are based," explains Reeves. "The profile of our customer base is also very diverse, so in that respect it makes sound business sense, for example, in an area where English is not the first language, to employ staff who are able to communicate with customers in their first language."

THE FUTURE

Reeves is aware that an ongoing recruitment programme of 14,000 high calibre new staff a year is no mean feat in an employment climate where potential recruits are in short supply in many areas, but is confident that the target is attainable. "We are already on course to achieve our recruitment goals for the expansion plan, but for such a large-scale exercise it does mean bearing in mind a number of points," she says.

"In the first place, you must be on the ball and know exactly where the potential labour market is positioned. Secondly, you need to be creative in your approach to attracting staff and exploit technology to its fullest potential. And finally, you must listen to your clients and the recruiters in the regions who have a grasp of what is happening on the ground."

Case study – B&Q

Chapter 16
Case study – Virginmoney.com

Online bank Virginmoney.com – "the place to sort out money" – was launched in June 2000. Through the internet it provides customers with access to a range of financial companies and products – such as ISAs (Individual Savings Accounts), mortgages and pensions – and search tools called "wizards" help customers trawl the internet to find the best deal. In its first year the company signed up more than 175,000 registered users – well ahead of plan.

The business concept was developed by the parent company's financial services arm, Virgin Direct, which sells own-brand investment, pension and life insurance products. "Regulations in force at the time meant that Virginmoney.com had to be set up completely separately from Virgin's other financial entities," explains Karen Thornber, head of HR with the internet business. But the two companies, based at a business park in Norwich, later merged when the regulations changed. This chapter looks at how the online banking business grew from its earliest days to the point of the merger.

THE IMPORTANCE OF BRAND

Virginmoney.com was built on the strong Virgin brand. As Karen Thornber comments: "We felt that there was a synergy between the internet and the Virgin brand that would help to build the success of the new company. Both can be described as entrepreneurial, energetic and fast-moving."

Thornber believes that the "big brand" and Virgin's reputation in the marketplace helped to attract the staff needed to resource the new business. "We had to recruit over 100, mainly specialist, people within a very short space of time," she says. "The internet industry is dynamic and competitive, so we needed to have in place an innovative recruitment and selection strategy."

A core of experienced and talented people transferred from Virgin Direct to set up the new venture. Karen Thornber herself was uniquely placed to manage the recruitment drive, having previously worked for Virgin and been involved in the development of other internet companies. A nucleus of existing Virgin staff has continued to work in the new company which, in Thornber's view, has helped to transpose and cement Virgin's distinctive corporate culture.

Case study – Virginmoney.com

USING A RECRUITMENT AGENCY

In view of the short timescale, the project team engaged the services of Icarus, a recruitment agency, for the early stages of the recruitment process. The agency ran an extensive advertising campaign and headhunted key individuals before providing a shortlist of candidates for each post. The shortlisting process was assisted by screening interviews that were recorded on video.

"The video interviewing was a very effective and fast way of initially screening candidates," says Thornber. "We at Virgin also made a video to play to candidates of different managers talking about the brand and what it is like working for the company – so the process was two-way."

Thornber advises other companies considering the use of a recruitment agency for a large-scale recruitment campaign to brief the agency very carefully on both the type of people required and the culture of the company. "Engaging a consultancy was absolutely necessary in view of the time pressure and it worked very well," she says. "But, in the later stages, we assumed complete responsibility for recruitment as there was a danger we were missing potential recruits. It is also more effective to have people who work in the company responsible for recruitment and selection, who know the culture and instinctively know what competencies we are looking for."

SELECTING FOR A CULTURE

After the initial screening process, Virgin staff interviewed the candidates, usually on a one-to-one basis. In view of the importance of recruiting people suited to Virgin's strong culture, face-to-face interviews were considered the most reliable way of making final selection decisions.

"Because we had a very clear vision of what we were trying to build with the new company, we also had an almost intuitive feel for getting the best people on board: those with a similar "can-do" mentality who relished a challenge and who were prepared to be flexible," says Thornber. For this reason, Virgin made a conscious decision not to undertake psychometric testing of candidates. The interviews were conducted on a formal basis, but were conversational and relaxed so that candidates were encouraged to communicate openly.

Recruiting the right staff often involved balancing the need for very technical and expert skills with the need for cultural fit. "The business environment we are operating in is changing constantly," explains Thornber. "We therefore need people with a certain mindset who are very open to change in their approach to work."

Very detailed and comprehensive role profiles were carefully developed to aid the recruitment and selection process. "I have learned from my previous experience of building new companies that it is essential to have in place at the outset a clearly defined management framework, with role profiles for all jobs, including behavioural competencies and the key job components," advises Karen Thornber.

She also believes that a flexible attitude on the part of employees is a prerequisite for successfully setting up a new business. The wisdom of this approach has been borne out already at Virginmoney, with some employees adapting to different roles, such as analysts switching to project management work. "We ourselves have had to tweak the original template for the company as it was growing," explains Karen Thornber. "Recruiting people who are not afraid of variance was therefore vital."

Virginmoney.com was launched with a workforce made up of 80% contractors, a figure that was reduced to 18% within six months. The common practice of subcontracting in the dotcom industry means that the company continues to operate with an element of contractors.

RECOMMEND A FRIEND

Another recruitment method that was used very successfully to resource the start-up company was Virgin's "recommend a friend" scheme. An employee who puts someone forward for a job is paid to the value of £1,500 in Virgin vouchers on completion of the new recruit's probationary period.

"The scheme is a very effective way of consolidating the culture – so important to Virgin," comments Thornber. "The fact that existing employees are recommending people they know is a strong indicator of fit with our values."

DEFINING THE CULTURE

Culture is integral to all Virgin's activities, including recruitment and selection. In Thornber's view, it is also the main reason why attrition is so low. "Only two permanent staff have left the organisation since it was launched," she says. "There is a real family feel in the company, it is very personable and the bottom line is that people enjoy working here – so they stay."

When asked to define the culture, Thornber describes it as "work hard/play hard and very open". As is customary in the dynamic and pressurised dotcom environment, employees do not necessarily work nine to five, but employees' social lives spill over into the office. "The age profile for the company is, typically for the sector, very young and we put a lot of emphasis on having fun," says Thornber. "We play basketball and have a sports day and even have snowball fights – we had a party in the park, or rather car park, and that was in work hours."

Aside from having fun, such activities are part of the company's conscious approach to recognising and valuing employees on an individual level. "These peripheral fun gestures, like a card and a bag of money on every person's desk to mark Virginmoney.com's first birthday, are an important way of reinforcing a caring and very personal culture," says Thornber.

NEW STARTERS

Induction for new recruits is considered an important conclusion to the recruitment process at Virginmoney. As well as a forum for imparting key company information and carrying out the administrative tasks necessary for commencing employment, induction also signals the beginning of employees' socialisation into Virginmoney.com.

To provide new starters with an overview of the business, a cross-section of existing employees were interviewed on video to recount their experiences of working for the company. This idea was developed further to mark Virginmoney's first birthday.

A "big brother" room was set up with a video recorder permanently in situ so that employees could enter and record their reflections on the first year of the company's life. The tapes – which according to Thornber featured observations from staff that were both humorous ("so-and-so doesn't make the coffee") and serious ("it has been very hard but rewarding work") – have subsequently been used as part of the induction process.

RETAINING STAFF

Although many internet companies focus on reward as a key mechanism for retaining staff, Thornber describes Virginmoney's reward package as "good, but mid-market for the industry". Employees are paid a basic salary, an annual bonus of between 10%–25% and a 5% company pension contribution. A long-term incentive scheme operates for employees and all staff receive discounts on Virgin products.

The project team made a conscious decision not to change the existing Virgin salary structure for the new venture. "There was definitely a pressure to adapt our reward package for the internet business, but I felt quite strongly that there are other, more effective ways of motivating and retaining staff," says Thornber.

She is a firm believer in a more intrinsic approach to satisfying employees' expectations at work: "I think people come to work wanting to do a good job and, therefore, we have created an enabling environment that aims to engage people's hearts and minds."

The company is prepared to invest in its employees to gain the loyalty needed to guarantee its success as a new venture. "It is definitely a two-way process," she says. "We need to connect with people on an almost emotional level to gain their commitment." Recognition can be demonstrated in small but personal ways, according to Thornber, such as a birthday card and prizes for successfully completing a task or project.

Virginmoney's supportive approach to managing people is reinforced by what Thornber describes as excellent training and career opportunities. "HR is not just a support function at Virginmoney," she continues. "It is an integral and strategic part of the business, especially in terms of what kind of people the company needs to make it happen. That therefore includes not only finding the right staff in the first place, but developing and encouraging them to succeed once they are in post."

Flexibility works both ways at Virginmoney.com, and although the length of the working day can easily exceed normal working hours, there is also a certain amount of leeway for staff to vary their working arrangements. Some staff work from home and there are no fixed start-and-finish times in the office.

SUCCESS IS MEASURABLE

Karen Thornber believes that there are hard measures to indicate that Virginmoney.com's recruitment and retention strategies contributed to its early succes. "As well as our almost negligible turnover rate, absence rates are incredibly low, which shows a real commitment to the goals of the business on the part of employees," she says.

She attributes the company's low attrition to several factors. It has put in place an effective and robust recruitment process, and has addressed key retention issues at an early stage, such as ensuring cultural fit with the company. A thorough induction programme has been introduced and Virginmoney has paid attention to the psychological issues that motivate people.

Karen Thornber has some specific words of advice for others considering a start-up venture. "In the first place, flexibility is the name of the game," she says. "As the new business develops, so you should maximise and develop the talents of your people, and that means understanding them first."

In her view, this requires a strong vision of what you are trying to achieve in the long term and the ability to remain focused. "Although the process of setting up Virginmoney was a rapid one, it was also an evolutionary progression and we needed to be adaptable," she says. Thornber is clear about the implications for the human resources function. "It is vital that the HR team understands exactly what the business requirements are," she advises. "It is also imperative that you manage people's expectations from the start, and manage upwards by involving employees."